FROM CASHBOX TO CLASSROOM

THE STRUGGLE FOR FISCAL REFORM AND EDUCATIONAL CHANGE IN NEW JERSEY

FROM CASHBOX TO CLASSROOM

THE STRUGGLE FOR FISCAL REFORM AND EDUCATIONAL CHANGE IN NEW JERSEY

William A. Firestone
Margaret E. Goertz
Gary Natriello

Teachers College, Columbia Universityy
New York and London

Published by Teachers College Press, 1234 Amsterdam Avenue, New York, N.Y. 10027

Library of Congress Cataloging-in-Publication Data
Firestone, William A.
    From cashbox to classroom : the struggle for fiscal reform and
educational change in New Jersey / William A. Firestone, Margaret E.
Goertz, Gary Natriello.
      p.   cm.
    Includes bibliographical references (p.) and index.
    ISBN 0-8077-3555-8 (pbk. : alk. paper)
    1. Education—New Jersey——Finance—Case studies. 2. Educational
change—New Jersey—Case studies. 3. Education and state—New
Jersey—Case studies. 4. Educational equalization—New Jersey—Case
studies. I. Goertz, Margaret E. II. Natriello, Gary. III. Title.
LB2826.N5F53   1997
379.749—dc21   97-26580

ISBN 0-8077-3555-8 (paper)

Printed on acid-free paper
Manufactured in the United States of America
04 03 02 01 00 99 98 97   8 7 6 5 4 3 2 1

CONTENTS

PREFACE

There was considerable optimism in New Jersey's liberal policy community in the spring of 1990. After 20 years of litigation and two law suits, the state supreme court had found that the school finance system was inequitable and had to be changed to better support children in urban schools. Moreover, because the newly elected Democratic governor was from the city of Camden and had a history of supporting urban issues, and because the legislature was solidly Democratic, there was reason to believe that the state's long-running school finance dispute might finally be resolved to the benefit of the state's poor children. Similar decisions in Kentucky and Texas suggested that New Jersey's situation was not unique.

While many people were excited about the possibilities, we had a more personal interest in the issue. It was not just that we all worked or lived in New Jersey. Margaret Goertz was an expert witness for the plaintiffs who filed the *Abbott* suit. Gary Natriello had been studying and writing on education for disadvantaged students and was an expert witness in a similar suit involving the Hartford, Connecticut schools. William Firestone had studied a wide range of school reforms and was starting an educational research center designed to address the central policy issues in the state.

We also saw another opportunity in the New Jersey situation. We felt that, in general, research on school finance was too disconnected from the work on educational reform. The first focused on how money was raised and distributed but paid too little attention to what it was spent on. The second examined the implementation and effects of whatever innovations were popular at the moment, but it rarely seriously examined the resources needed to implement these reforms or the reasons why the reforms were so much more frequent in suburban areas than in urban areas. Many questions remained unresolved: What does money buy? Is it worth spending more in urban schools? How do we make schools both more efficient and effective?

We thought, working as a team, we could help bridge this gap. The three of us together possess expertise in all the levels of the school system, from the state house to the classroom. Professor Goertz's training is in policy, and she had concentrated on issues of school finance. Professors Firestone and

Natriello are both educational sociologists with a strong interest in organizational behavior. Firestone had studied school administration and how reforms affect teachers. Natriello had looked at the work of teachers and how larger social and educational forces affect poor children. We thought that if anyone could do a study that went beyond conventional school finance to explore how changing revenues affected educational practice and the way that local districts translated state financial policy into the delivery of services, we should be able to. Because the team was so diverse and the task was so broad, we felt that we would be breaking new ground.

Reality caught up with us very quickly. The political backlash to the school finance reform began even before funding for the study was assured. Early on the New Jersey legislature began to back away from its initial commitment. The changing political climate created new challenges and frustrations for us: how to evaluate the impact of a changing law; how to share our findings with an increasingly disinterested group of state policy makers; how to balance our roles as social science researchers and as individuals concerned about the well-being of the state's poor children and its educational system; and how to share the positive findings of this work with the New Jersey Supreme Court since we had pledged anonymity to our study districts.

After this book was completed, on December 20, 1996, the New Jersey legislature enacted still another school funding law, the Comprehensive Educational Improvement and Financing Act (CEIFA). The *Abbott* plaintiffs returned to court immediately to challenge the constitutionality of this new law that purports to link education funding to the state's new Core Curriculum Content Standards. The plaintiffs charged that CEIFA fails to assure parity in regular education expenditures and to provide adequate supplemental programs, as mandated by the court in 1990 and again in 1994.

The court ruled in favor of the plaintiffs in May 1997, and Governor Whitman and the legislature allocated an additional $246 million to the state's poor urban school districts. The justices also ordered the commissioner of education to develop a plan to address the special educational and facilities needs of these communities. We believe that our research has much to say about how school leaders have and can make effective use of these new resources. We hope that this book will help educators, policy makers, and the public throughout the country better understand the processes by which revenues get turned into services for children and, thereby, help make all our schools more equitable, efficient, and excellent.

William A. Firestone
Margaret E. Goertz
Gary J. Natriello

ACKNOWLEDGMENTS

We are grateful to the many people who assisted in the study and the preparation of this book. Our work would not have been possible without the outstanding cooperation of the teachers, principals, and district administrators in our twelve study districts. They welcomed us into their schools and classrooms for three consecutive years, patiently answering our many questions. The insights and information they provided us were invaluable. We also thank the many superintendents throughout New Jersey who responded to our two statewide surveys, and the staff of the New Jersey State Department of Education who gave us background information on the design and implementation of the Quality Education Act and other state education policies.

We are indebted to Beverly Hetrick, Brianna Nagle, and Marcy Smelkinson who were principal site visitors in several of our districts and played a major role in the development of district case studies and in our cross-site analysis work. Jeannette DeJesus, Frances Lakis, Tom Bowers, and Bonnie Kroll also assisted us in data collection. Kroll and Bowers painstakingly analyzed the district budget and staffing data, respectively, while Morgan Collins prepared the data files for the teacher and superintendent surveys.

Robb Sewell and Amy Brown held the office together and kept us organized while we chased after interviews, observations, and documents from all over the state. This book was greatly strengthened by the comments of outside reviewers and by Susan Liddicoat of Teachers College Press.

Finally, financial and moral support for the study came from three foundations and their program officers—Stephanie Bell-Rose at the Mellon Foundation, Lallie O'Brien at the Pew Charitable Trusts, and Marla Ucelli at the Rockefeller Foundation—who are committed to improving educational opportunities for poor children and believe that research can contribute to better education policy and practice. This book does not necessarily reflect the position or policies of these organizations or individuals, however. We take collective responsibility for the findings and views presented in the following pages.

1

INTRODUCTION

S chool finance reform is one of the most contentious issues to face educators and state policy makers since desegregation. Over the last 25 years, education finance systems have been challenged in 34 states, sometimes more than once, because of spending disparities between rich and poor districts. Courts declared school finance systems unconstitutional in 15 states and litigation remains unresolved in another dozen states (Hickrod, 1991; Verstegen, 1994).

A court mandate, no matter how strong, is only the starting point in implementing school finance reform. Decisions on how to formulate a more equitable system of funding education are ultimately the responsibility of the state legislature. The design and enactment of reform legislation is a complex task that requires consensus on such philosophical questions as the meaning of equality of educational opportunity, the appropriate balance between the state's constitutional responsibility for education and local control, how much a good education should cost, and who should pay the bill. Education funding decisions are also intertwined with broader tax policy issues. The public, dissatisfied with rising property taxes, wants the state to play a larger role in the funding of public education. At the same time, state policy makers are being pressured to reduce or stabilize state taxes and spending.

New Jersey illustrates the conflicts that school finance litigation can generate. In June 1990, after nine years of litigation, the state supreme court declared New Jersey's school finance law unconsitutional (*Abbott v Burke,* 119 N.J. 287, herein referenced as *Abbott II*). This decision did not invalidate the entire state school finance system, but it required that more resources go to poor urban districts than to wealthy suburban ones:

> It is clear ... that in order to achieve the constitutional standard for the student from these poorer urban districts ..., the totality of the district's educational offerings must contain elements over and above those found in the affluent suburban district. If the educational fare of the seriously disadvantaged student is the same as the "regular education" given to the advantaged student, those serious disadvantages will not be addressed, and students in the poorer urban districts will simply not be able to compete. (*Abbott II* at 374)

With little discussion outside the State House and little opposition within his own party, newly elected Governor Jim Florio, an advocate for the state's cities, and the state Democratic leadership pushed the Quality Education Act (QEA I) through the legislature the month following the court's decision. A major purpose of the bill was to reduce expenditure disparities between the state's 30 poorest urban communities and its 108 wealthiest districts, as mandated by the court. This legislation increased state education aid by $1.15 billion, established a foundation level of $6,835 per pupil, and increased support for students with special educational needs. Legislators also enacted a $2.8 billion tax package to fund the QEA I, address a projected budget deficit, and provide local property tax relief.

Opposition to these tax and education finance bills was immense and formed even before the QEA I was signed into law. Motorcades converged on the state capitol. The governor's approval rating dropped 19 points, and those who ranked his performance as poor more than doubled from 14% to 32% ("Tax Hikes," 1990). The depth of this opposition became apparent in the fall of 1990 when Democrat Bill Bradley, a popular U.S. Senator, nearly lost re-election to an unknown Republican challenger.

Most opposition was to the tax increases, but some was directed at the new school funding law. A poll taken shortly after the QEA was enacted found that 56% of New Jerseyans opposed it while 35% supported the legislation ("Most New Jerseyans," 1990). While the major worry was that the QEA would raise taxes, two more specific concerns were expressed. The first concern was that additional funds would be wasted in the urban districts:

> The state of New Jersey has a program of compensatory education. The federal government has its Title I funding. These programs have poured millions upon millions of dollars into various school systems with little, if any, effect. (Hrevnack, 1991)

> And frankly it is hard to avoid the suspicion that, at this frenzied pace, the money won't be carefully directed, but will be shoveled hastily into the bottomless pit of New Jersey's disaster areas. (Sacks, 1990)

> The court is requiring working-class people residing in middle-income communities who drive around in Fords to buy Mercedes for people in the poorest cities because they don't have cars. ("Decision Draws Mixed Reaction," 1990)

The second fear was that increased aid to the poorest school districts would come at the expense of richer ones:

> The dolorous result [of the QEA] is that it could create serious problems for suburban schools by diluting the quality of education in those districts. . . . While it was the intent of both the Supreme Court and the Legislature to redress the funding of urban schools, it was surely not intended by either branch of government to do so by seriously undermining the viable continuity of delivering quality schooling for suburban children. ("Viewpoint," 1990)

> Democratic Assemblyman Daniel P. Jacobson . . . summed up the situation by saying that the legislature had to "strike a balance between the middle-class taxpayers—the struggling taxpayers—and the kid who through no fault of his own had to go to an [urban] school that nobody wants him to. . . . " Jacobson complained that the law seemed to be "punitive" in withdrawing state money from his Shore district's affluent schools. ("School Debate," 1990)

The Democratic legislative leadership soon distanced itself from Florio's original proposals and amended the QEA in March 1991, 4 months before the original law was to take effect. The new bill, dubbed the QEA II, reduced the increase in state education aid from $1.15 billion to $800 million, reduced the base foundation level by nearly $200 per pupil, and made a number of other changes designed to provide direct relief to the state's taxpayers. But these changes were too little and too late. The Democrats lost control of both houses of the state legislature by an overwhelming margin in the November 1991 elections. Governor Florio lost his bid for re-election 2 years later.

Debates over school finance reform are so heated because they bring to the surface tensions among three basic values in education: equity, efficiency, and excellence. Advocates of school finance reform seek to maximize the educational opportunities for all children by equalizing the funding of education. This approach is usually accompanied by increased spending, which conflicts with the beliefs of many that schools do not need more money, but rather need to use existing resources more efficiently. A recurring third theme in American education is the search for excellence, most recently expressed as the imperative to make American schools and school children more internationally competitive. Yet, discussions of higher educational standards are rarely accompanied by discussions of how much quality education costs or how it should be funded.

These conflicting values come to the forefront when policy makers design education reform policies. How much money should be spent on education to provide quality services to all students? What aspects of the educational program should be equalized? How can the state ensure the most efficient and effective use of public dollars? Guthrie (1980) argues, however, that "isolated pursuit of any one value is virtually impossible. . . . The coalition building necessary to define, fashion, and implement a widespread reform almost always necessitates concessions to proponents of yet another value stream" (p. 40).

This book uses the experiences of New Jersey to inform the design of more equitable, efficient, and effective state school finance systems. Using a combination of traditional school finance equity analyses, in-depth case studies of 12 school districts, and statewide surveys and databases, we examine the extent to which New Jersey's 1990 school finance reform equalized both education revenues and school districts' capacities to deliver quality education. We identify the fiscal and nonfiscal factors that contributed to the changes (or lack of change) that we observed. And we examine how the three values of equity, efficiency, and excellence are embodied in state policies; how they interact; and how they impact education reform efforts.

The remainder of this chapter introduces the concepts of equity, efficiency, and excellence as they apply to education finance policy; presents the three major research questions that frame our study; summarizes our research methodology; and provides a brief overview of the rest of the book.

THE THREE Es

Debates over how to operationalize equity, efficiency, and excellence precede the history of school finance reform and may be as old as the Republic itself. Although the post-World War II periods of education reform have been portrayed as focusing on one or another of these values, untangling efforts to achieve, for example, equity, from those directed at maximizing efficiency or excellence at any point in time is difficult (Guthrie, 1980). Our purpose here is to describe how these three values have been embodied in education reform initiatives over the last 40 years and to identify ways in which these values interact in education finance litigation, policy, and research.

Equity

Equity has been a theme in American policy making since the Declaration of Independence held "these truths to be self evident, that all men are created equal." Yet, Americans have always been ambivalent about equity. While most Americans agree that education is important for giving all children an equal opportunity to succeed, they always want their own children's chances to be a little more equal (Cohen & Neufeld, 1981).

The Supreme Court's 1954 decision *Brown v Board of Education* put equity center stage in education policy debates. Yet, even though major strides were made through the 1964 Civil Rights Act and the Elementary and Secondary

Education Act of 1965, substantial inequities in educational opportunities remained. Attention expanded from desegregation to the allocation of educational resources as scholars began to document the funding inequities between rich and poor districts that stemmed from the extensive use of local property taxes to support education (Guthrie, 1980). Some of these scholars (Coons, Clune, & Sugarman, 1970; Wise, 1968) concluded that rich districts had too much political influence for these inequities to be alleviated through the legislative process, and they proposed legal theories to challenge school funding arrangements in both federal and state courts. With the publication of their work, a loose network of civil rights attorneys, legal scholars, and social scientists began developing litigation strategies and mounting suits challenging existing inequities.

The first wave of litigants grounded their arguments for equal funding for all children in the equal protection clause of the U. S. Constitution. Their claim, that variations in education revenues that were a function of district wealth violated the federal equal protection clause, was rejected in 1973 by the U.S. Supreme Court in *San Antonio v Rodriguez*. In a 5-to-4 decision, the Court ruled that since education was not mentioned in the U. S. Constitution, it did not constitute a fundamental right that must be provided equally to all students.

After the *Rodriguez* decision, attention shifted to the state courts with pleadings alleging violations of the education and equal protection clauses of state constitutions. Education is explicitly designated a state responsibility in state constitutions, although the wording of these guarantees varies across states. Attorneys use education clauses in two ways to challenge the constitutionality of their states' school finance systems. First, they argue that an unequal distribution of education resources violates the state's responsibility to provide all children the constitutionally guaranteed "basic," "adequate," or "thorough and efficient" education. Second, they use education clauses to establish education as a fundamental right in the state, subjecting the review of state school finance systems to "strict scrutiny" under state equal protection clauses. Under this test, state funding structures must serve a compelling state interest to pass constitutional muster.

Courts have used their authority to interpret state education clauses to define the scope and substance of states' responsibilities for education and the degree and type of equity required of school funding systems. One cannot predict the outcome of school finance cases from the wording of education clauses, however. Instead, success depends on a combination of the language of these provisions, the states' constitutional and legal history, and the activism of the state justices (Underwood, 1994). Verstegen (1994) speculates that courts are more willing to invalidate school finance laws using education rather than equal protection clauses because decisions reached about schools will not apply to other government services.

Equity and efficiency arguments have interacted from the beginning of the legal challenges. In many cases, defendants used data from education production function studies to argue that more money will not translate into higher test scores (e.g., *Abbott v Burke, Harper v Hunt*). No court has overturned an inequitable school funding system without first finding a positive relationship between expenditures and educational opportunity (Dayton, 1993). For example, the Kentucky court found that spending disparities between poor and wealthy school districts led to differences on a number of indicators of education quality *(Rose v The Council for Better Schools)*. The New Jersey Supreme Court similarly argued that money makes a difference in the quality of education. The justices reasoned that money buys improved staff ratios, higher teacher salaries, expanded programs, more equipment, and better facilities. "If these factors are *not* related to the quality of education, why are the richer districts willing to spend so much for them?" *(Abbott II* at 368)

The notion of educational excellence has been raised in school finance equity cases in two ways. First, plaintiffs alleging that expenditure disparities between school districts are unconstitutional (funding equity claims) often make their case by showing the negative effects of inadequate funding levels on the quality and quantity of educational services and programs available to students. Second, litigation is increasingly focused on the adequacy, as well as equity, of school finance systems. Adequacy theories hold that students are entitled to receive an education that will prepare them to be both informed citizens and skilled and productive workers in a competitive economy. In educational adequacy claims, plaintiffs first seek a ruling that their state constitution guarantees all students an adequate education. The state's funding system can then be found unconstitutional if the state does not provide an adequate education—as defined in its constitution, laws, and policies, or by other contemporary standards (Minorini, 1994; Morgan, Cohen, & Hershkoff, 1995).

Lawsuits have been the most effective way of advancing the school finance equity agenda, but because equity is a redistributive issue, both the court cases and the politics of passing and implementing legislation are highly contentious (Peterson, Rabe, & Wong, 1988). Support for policies to equalize spending between districts has been undermined by 20 years or more of "white flight" from the cities to suburban areas of at least moderate wealth. Most middle and upper income voters have little interest in providing more funding for poorer districts, perhaps especially those where the students are racially different (e.g., Wong, 1994). There is no agreement in our society on the need to provide even minimum living standards to children, much less equal educational opportunity (Orfield, 1994a). Policies to move toward statewide support for education are usually voted down (Wong, 1994), and court-mandated equalization policies often generate heated opposition.

Nevertheless, in spite of varying degrees of opposition, state legislatures have reformed their school finance systems. Between 1970 and 1980, 28 states enacted new or revised education aid programs; 12 of these reforms were in response to court cases. State education expenditures nearly tripled in nominal dollars, and states enacted or expanded programs for students with special needs (Odden & Augenblick, 1981). The state share of educational revenue rose from 40% in 1970 to nearly 50% in 1986, and has hovered around 47% since the late 1980s (National Center for Education Statistics, 1995). As the states' contribution to education increased, legislatures becoame more active in the education policy arena. This increased spending also motivated legislators' interest in both efficiency and excellence.

Efficiency

Efforts to promote efficiency in education date back at least to efforts to rationalize school administration through the application of scientific management principles and the formation of school districts in the late 19th century (Tyack, 1974). In the last 30 years, three streams of academic research have shaped thinking about efficiency. These have focused on how much money is spent on education, whether money makes a difference in student performance, and whether money is spent wisely.

First, research has documented that the cost of education, even when adjusted for inflation and changes in student enrollments, has been growing since the turn of the century (Hanushek et al., 1994). The per-pupil cost of education grew 69% in the 1960s, 35% in the 1970s, and 35% in the 1980s, although part of this increase reflected funding for new services for poor, disabled, and other special needs students. Per-pupil spending was relatively flat in the early 1990s, however (Lankford & Wyckoff, 1995; Odden, Monk, Nakib, & Picus, 1995).

The second line of research examines how education resources are related to student outcomes. Coleman et al. (1966) were the first to systematically document the large impact of nonschool conditions, especially family background, on student learning. The school factors that made a difference were often of the sort that could not be purchased, such as the composition of the student body. Since then an extensive body of research, often borrowing from economic theory, has sought to identify a "production function" that would specify the inputs that contribute to student achievement. Research in this tradition has shown the strong effects of individual background on student learning (Natriello, McDill, & Pallas, 1990). The contribution of financial inputs to student learning in general and the potential for increased revenue to overcome the effects of family background have been hotly debated. Analysts disagree on how to interpret the same studies (Hanushek, 1989; Hedges, Laine, & Greenwald, 1994) and question the relevance of this entire line of work to the debate over equalizing funding (Murnane, 1991).

Nevertheless, evidence of a tenuous relationship between spending and student learning challenged the assumptions of equity advocates that equalizing spending between rich and poor districts would reduce the achievement gap between rich and poor students. The production function research lent credence to the public concerns noted earlier in this chapter that large increases of funds to poor school districts would be wasted. Others argued that added funding would lead only to increased benefits for teachers with little change in services for students (see, for example, Moynihan, 1972) or would be consumed by an "administrative blob" rather than being directed to the instruction of children.

A third line of research has emerged that examines the question of how school districts use their funds, paying particular attention to how much money is directed to the classroom and to the instruction of students. Here it is assumed that efficiency is increased by concentrating resources at the classroom level. One set of studies has used statewide data to determine how much of the education dollar is spent on instruction, administration, and other services. Regardless of district size, socioeconomic composition, urbanicity, or spending level, districts spend their resources in similar ways: about 60% of their budgets on instruction and another 8% to 10% on instructional supports (such as student services, curriculum development, and professional development). Administrative expenditures account for less than 10% of the budget, and in most cases at least half of this amount is spent at the school level (Odden et al., 1995). A second set of studies looks within districts to determine how much is spent at the school and classroom levels. Analyses of budgets in a small number of districts showed that about 90% of their resources were spent at the school level, and 55% to 60% in the classroom (Cooper et al., 1994).

Three criticisms of these research literatures, especially the production function research, have implications for future research on, and for policies designed to maximize, the impact of new education dollars on poor students and school districts. First, the outcome measures used in these studies are generally limited to test scores that provide limited criteria for what most people expect children to learn in school. In the past, by focusing on basic skills, these tests ignored some of the most important creative capacities that children will need in a modern, fast changing society (Madaus, 1988). A new wave of authentic or performance-based assessments appears to tap a wider variety of thinking skills, but it is difficult to imagine "testing" some of the moral development outcomes—from punctuality to "effective citizenship"—that people hope schools will help engender.

Second, these studies have used narrow, underdeveloped theories of learning that emphasize variables that can be included in large-scale data analyses and are closely linked to funding. Variables like class size, teachers' education or even their verbal capacity, while amenable to large-scale measurement, may not predict student learning as well as instructional strategy, content coverage, or the interaction of such factors with student ability or background knowledge (Gamoran, 1989; Monk, 1992). Such work can result in a simplistic, mechanistic description of the relationship between spending and student learning. Moreover, it does not deal with legitimate, non-learning outcomes of schooling that have costs. Taxpayers and parents expect schools to provide everything from student safety to sources of community solidarity (Johnson, 1995; Peshkin, 1984); these concerns are not reflected in discussions about relationships between revenues and student learning.

Finally, and most important for this study, most of this research is cross-sectional, involving data collected at a single point in time. Thus it provides little information on how changes in revenues are translated in changed educational opportunities for students (Monk, 1992). One possibility is that school districts with limited revenues have a backlog of pent-up demands, proposals based on local needs that had been cut out of the budget for lack of resources. In such districts there may be clear consensus on which priorities to address first when revenues increase (Kirst, 1977). Nor does existing research consider how other factors, such as enrollment changes or increases in expensive-to-educate students, absorb new education dollars (Lankford & Wyckoff, 1995). Thus, the hypotheses that *increased* education funds will be wasted, or that they will put to good use, are both based on slim evidence.

Policy makers have adopted three strategies to improve the efficiency of their educational systems. The first involves a continued focus on better management practices through the introduction of such management tools as Program Performance Budgeting Systems (PPBS), Management by Objectives (MBO), and performance contracting (Guthrie, 1980). The second strategy is designed to force the more efficient use of resources by limiting the amount of public money school districts can raise or spend on education. Perhaps the best -known tax limitation policies are Proposition 13 in California and Proposition 2 1/2 in Massachusetts, both state constitutional amendments enacted in the late 1970s that cap local property tax rates. But 43 states impose some type of limitation on school taxes and/or spending, or revenues (Mullins & Cox, as cited in Gold, Smith, & Lawton, 1995).

The third approach to promote efficiency is to hold schools and school districts accountable for the performance of their students. Accountability systems have traditionally focused on educational inputs and administrative processes. As states pay increased attention to student standards, they are revising their accountability systems to focus more heavily on student performance and the process of teaching and learning at the school level. Although there are few performance-based systems in operation, those in place and under development in states like Kentucky and Maryland include a set of student outcome and performance standards, mechanisms for assessing student performance and progress (generally standardized tests and other assessments), and policies for using student outcome data to develop educational improvement plans, generate financial rewards and/, or impose sanctions, such as state takeover.

Excellence

The search for excellence in American education is a recurring response to national crises. Unlike equity, which focuses on differences among students, schools, and school districts, and efficiency, which attends to operations and costs, the excellence movement concentrates on increasing the scope and rigor of educational programs so that students are better prepared to respond to the identified threat. For example, after the Soviets launched Sputnik in 1957, the federal government enacted the National Defense Education Act and funded the National Science Foundation's curriculum development efforts in mathematics and science.

More recently, education reforms have been driven by concerns that students in the United States are not prepared to meet the demands of a technological society or to maintain the nation's competitive economic position internationally. In response to declining test scores in the late 1960s and 1970s, numerous commissions analyzed the problems of the American educational system and recommended reforms (Passow, 1984). These commissions also began to form a more challenging definition of what schools should accomplish. The most famous of the reports, *A Nation at Risk* (National Commission on Excellence in Education, 1983), defined school excellence as "high expectations and goals for all learners" (p. 12). In 1989, President Bush and the nation's governors embraced the concept of national education goals that include school readiness, academic competency, and preparation for responsible citizenship and productive employment (National Education Goals Panel, 1994).

The immediate response to the recommendations of both national and state commissions was an intensification of existing educational processes through more testing of students, increased course work requirements for high school graduation, and more rigorous teacher certification standards (Firestone, Fuhrman, & Kirst, 1993). Gradually, a new policy approach emerged that reflected a more complex conception of student achievement and a more sophisticated view of the policy structure needed to achieve that conception. The new conception of achievement moved beyond the basic skills movement of the 1970s to emphasize both more advanced topics and such higher order skills as problem solving and critical thinking. Foreshadowed by the work of John Dewey, this new view was grounded in the psychological research of Jean Piaget and the cognitive scientists (Cole, 1990).

The policy strategy, variously called *systemic reform* (Smith & O'Day, 1991), *instructional guidance* (Cohen & Spillane, 1993), and *standards-based reform* (McLaughlin, Shepard & O'Day, 1995), calls for states to align a variety of policy instruments around a set of high standards that embody the new conception of student learning. By 1995, every state but one was engaged in developing content standards, and states were, to varying extents, coordinating curricular frameworks and policies governing textbooks, assessment, instructional materials, and preservice training and professional development for teachers around those standards (Massell, Kirst, & Hoppe, 1997; Massell & Fuhrman, 1994). As states develop new and challenging standards for student learning, they can draw on the work of nearly a dozen national subject-matter associations for guidance. Since the National Council of Teachers of Mathematics (NCTM) issued new curriculum standards in mathematics in 1989, standards have been issued in either draft or final form in the arts, civics, foreign language, geography, health, history, music, physical education, science, and social studies.

The 1980s and 1990s saw a major effort not only to build tougher content into state tests but also to experiment with alternative formats that challenged students to demonstrate their communication skills and critical, problem-solving capacities (Council of Chief State School Officers, 1994; Murnane & Levy, 1996). This change has been driven by arguments that the minimum competency testing of the 1970s "dumbed down" the curriculum, so that what was supposed to be a minimum became a maximum for many students, especially those in poor and urban school systems (Madaus, 1988).

A concern for excellence intersects with issues of equity and efficiency in three ways. First, the current education reform movement calls for higher standards for *all* students. Most states include statements to this effect in their new standards documents and education improvement plans, although only a few have taken steps to hold their schools and school districts accountable for the performance of all students on these new goals. The most recent reauthorization of the federal program for educationally disadvantaged children, the Improving America's Schools Act of 1994 (Riley, 1995), requires states to include disadvantaged children in the implementation of higher standards.

Second, state courts have begun to link school finance equity and high student standards through the wave of educational adequacy cases. In states such as Alabama, Kentucky, and Massachusetts, courts have defined a constitutionally adequate and equitable public school system as one that provides students with the opportunity to attain specific skills that are necessary for them to be nationally and internationally competitive (Morgan, Cohen, & Hershkoff, 1995). Courts then require state legislatures to develop student performance standards for these skills and design a school finance system that assures adequate resources to educate all students to these standards.

Third, concerned that disadvantaged students would not have access to the kinds and level of educational programs needed to help them achieve higher standards, equity advocates have pushed for the development of *opportunity to learn standards* (Smith, Fuhrman, & O'Day, 1994). These standards would define a set of conditions that schools, districts, and states must meet to ensure that all students have the opportunity to learn the knowledge and skills embodied in the new content and performance standards. There is disagreement within the research and policy communities, however, about the focus of these standards (e.g., on the level and type of resources or on the way in which schools use resources to promote student learning) and about appropriate strategies for ensuring equal educational opportunities (Elmore & Fuhrman, 1995; Porter, 1993).

RESEARCH QUESTIONS

These themes and the nature of school finance reform policy suggest three questions that frame a study of the effects of school finance reform. By answering them we can offer guidance to policy makers for future efforts to maximize equity, efficiency, and excellence. At the same time, we are able to clarify how these different values interact and impact reform efforts.

1. TO WHAT EXTENT DID NEW JERSEY'S SCHOOL FINANCE REFORM, THE QUALITY EDUCATION ACT, EQUALIZE REVENUES AND EXPENDITURES BETWEEN RICH AND POOR DISTRICTS?

This is the traditional equity question raised by school finance scholars and the primary issued raised by the court in the *Abbott v Burke* litigation. Moreover, if the reform did not take significant steps towards such equalization, questions about the impact of school finance reform become moot. We use standard equity measures (Berne & Steifel, 1984) and fiscal data routinely collected by the New Jersey State Department of Education (SDE) to examine the extent to which the QEA reduced expenditure disparities between 1990/91 and 1993/94 and addressed the special educational needs of poor urban districts. We also identify factors that limited the equalizing impact of the reform law.

2. DID CHANGED EXPENDITURE PATTERNS EQUALIZE DISTRICTS' CAPACITIES TO PROVIDE A QUALITY EDUCATION TO STUDENTS?

The primary purpose of school finance reform is to equalize educational opportunities for children. Yet, we know little about whether and how equalization of dollars translates into enhanced educational services. In this study, we examine how changes in New Jersey's school finance system impacted four educational capacities that research shows affect student learning: personnel, curriculum and instruction, social services, and buildings and facilities.

Personnel is important for several reasons. First, the bulk of school operating budgets is allocated to both instructional and non-instructional personnel costs (Raimondo, 1994). Second, most predictions that augmenting school
district revenues is wasteful focus on personnel spending; critics argue that
new dollars will be used only to increase teacher salaries and/or increase the
number of administrators in the district. Finally, much of the research on the
relationships between expenditures and student learning (e.g., Hanushek, 1989)
focuses on such personnel variables as pupil-teacher ratios, teacher salaries,
and the interaction between teacher salaries and teacher characteristics such
as experience, further education, and verbal ability (Ferguson, 1991).

Criticisms of production function research (Monk, 1992) and the newer
work on instructional guidance (Cohen & Spillane, 1993) and opportunity-to-
learn (Porter, 1993) suggest that particularly for explaining student achievement,
information on personnel is not enough. It is also important to understand the
curriculum schools offer and how instruction is conducted. Textbooks, instructional materials, and professional development may not be a large part of the
district budget. However, decisions about what to teach and how are likely to
be the missing factors that determine how well teachers and administrators contribute to student learning, and these decisions are operationalized in large
measure through the provision of materials and professional development.

While teaching has been the conventional task of schooling, it, too, may
be insufficient to equalize educational opportunity. The importance of family
background to student learning suggests that other factors must be considered. Coleman (1987) argues that schools of whatever quality are more effective for children who bring extensive social capital with them, and that such
capital—in the form of attitudes, self-concepts, and networks—is much more
extensive in wealthy than in poor communities (Wilson, 1987). If that is true,
providing more and better-refined, cognitively oriented instruction will not
be sufficient to help a large portion of children, particularly the poorest.
Conventional educational services will need to be supplemented by a variety
of social and health services. There is a long-standing tradition of providing
students with minimal physical examinations, subsidized lunches, and some
psychological services in schools; but recently, this has expanded to include
a wider variety of services as well as an extended range of relationships with
parents (e.g., Epstein, 1992). Given the current distribution of social capital,
one would expect to find a greater need for social services in communities
serving the poor, thus creating an added cost in these school districts.

The fourth capacity concerns facilities and the maintenance of these buildings. The quality of facilities can clearly affect students' safety and their access
to curriculum and instruction; some districts in our study could not add new
teachers or services because they lacked the space to house them. Facilities also

have symbolic value, signaling how much the community or larger society values education and their students (Deal & Kennedy, 1982). Thus, the quality of facilities may relate to students' self-concept and willingness to stay in school.

It is relatively easy to track changes in spending per pupil and fiscal disparities over time. We tried to track changes in these four capacities as well. In many cases, however, the necessary data were not available to document conditions prior to the passage of the QEA. To the extent possible, we examined what conditions were like before school finance reform, what kinds of changes were being made, and what things were like 3 years later.

3. WHAT FACTORS INFLUENCED THE CHANGES IN EDUCATIONAL CAPACITIES IDENTIFIED?

The design, enactment, and implementation of education reform takes place in a fragmented governance system (Cohen & Spillane, 1993). As a result, we have come to view the policy process as an "ecology of games"—that is, a series of games that are interdependent and only loosely linked (Firestone, 1989). School finance reform comprises at least four such games: the court, state politics, state policy, and local administration. Each game is played on its own terms with its own rules, scoring procedures, and winners and losers. However, each depends on other games for resources, regulations, demands, and so forth. Thus, the state politics game provides the state administrative game with funds and policies to administer, while feedback from how those funds and policies are administered provides issues for the state politics game to address. Similarly the state policy game provides resources and constraints that affect how the local administration game is played, but local administrators then make demands on all three other games. No game stands alone, but each is only tangentially related to any of the others.

While the ecology of games perspective is useful for sensitizing policy analysts and policy makers to the complex interactions through which policy is made and implemented, a more focused application is needed to help explain how a legal decision can lead to changed capacities to educate students. Figure 1.1 provides an orienting framework that illustrates the connections among the various actors and conditions that might affect the delivery of educational services. The court decision is shown at the top of the figure; the capacities of local districts are represented at the bottom.

The most proximate influence on these capacities is not the court, but the local district context that includes the status of those capacities before the decision was reached, spending levels and patterns before and after the court decision, and the administrative context that influences how changed resources are translated into changed capacities. The district responds to two contexts. One is the community that provides students and funding based on available property wealth and community support. The other is the

FIGURE 1.1. *Model of factors affecting change in district capacities.*

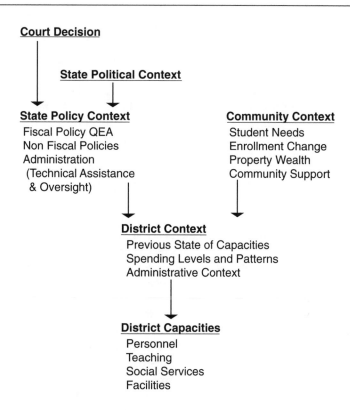

state policy context. This includes fiscal policy (as represented here by the QEA) and nonfiscal policies—including state tests, professional development, and curriculum specifications. It also encompasses the way the SDE administers these policies, including oversight and technical assistance provided to districts.

The state policy context is influenced most directly by the political context, decisions made by the legislature and the governor. These include specific pieces of legislation like the QEA and formal and informal efforts to influence the way the State Department of Education does its work. Finally, the political context is influenced by court decisions, which set an agenda for the legislature but leave considerable ambiguity on how to proceed.

We address issues of equity, efficiency, and excellence as they are represented in the various aspects of this framework. We show, for example, how these values are reflected and interact in the court decision, in the state policy context, and in New Jersey's education policies. Our assessment of the four district capacities provides some measure of the educational quality of a particular district, while cross-district comparison of these capacities shows the extent to which equity has been achieved. Examination of community fiscal and student inputs provides another perspective on educational equity. An exploration of patterns of spending and the processes by which new resources are transformed into changed district capacities provides some insight into district efficiency. Finally, an examination of the interaction of the state policy context and the local district context helps clarify the contribution the state can make to achieving all three values.

STUDY METHODOLOGY

We used a combination of qualitative and quantitative research methods to address these three questions. At the heart of this study are longitudinal case studies of 12 New Jersey school districts. Our sample of districts for the case studies reflected the categories of districts recognized in the QEA itself.

The QEA recognized three sets of local schools districts. The first, known as *Special Needs Districts*, included the original 28 districts identified by the state supreme court decision as well as two others added by the legislature. These districts, slated to receive additional funding under QEA, were poor and generally urban. Included in this set are some of the largest districts in the state, districts in small cities whose industrial bases had crumbled following World War II, and districts in small towns in the southern part of the state.

Because the special needs districts typically had records of poor student performance and because they were scheduled to receive additional state funds under the QEA, they became the focus of the most general public concern. While proponents of the QEA hoped that the additional resources would enable these districts to improve conditions for student learning, critics of the legislation suspected that these resources would only lead to further inefficiency and wasted public resources.

Since the overriding questions about the QEA concerned the performance of these special needs districts, half of our case study districts were drawn from these 30. These six districts, identified here as SN1 through SN6 in this volume, represent a 20% sample of the special needs districts. The six districts were selected to represent different geographic regions of the state,: north, central, and south. They range in size from under 5,000 students to over 25,000 students, and include some of the largest and poorest districts in the state with the highest concentrations of minority students.

The supreme court identified 108 wealthy districts as the group whose spending patterns would serve as the criterion to be achieved by the special needs districts in any new legislation to equalize spending. The QEA removed state general education funding from these districts, but, as part of a compromise in the legislature, provided state funds for a transition period to allow these districts to adjust their spending. Most *Transition Aid Districts* were among the 108 wealthiest in the state. These districts are scattered throughout the state and tend to be small.

Second in public concern only to the worry about waste in the special needs districts was the possibility of a decline of quality in the transition aid districts. QEA sponsors argued that the transition aid districts could deal with a reduction in state aid without negative effects on the quality of education provided; critics charged that the reduction would seriously erode educational quality. Four of our case study districts are drawn from the 108 districts in the transition aid category. These districts are identified as TR1 through TR4. Like the special needs districts in our sample, they were drawn from different geographic locations. Since most transition aid districts were smaller, the districts in our sample range in size from about 2,000 students to about 5,000 students.

The remainder of the more than 500 local school districts in New Jersey not identified as among either the 30 special needs districts or the 108 transition aid districts are those that continue to receive foundation aid under the QEA. These *Foundation Aid Districts* range widely in size, community wealth, and student demographics. For the most part they are neither very wealthy nor very poor, though, of course, some resemble special needs districts and others are similar to transition aid districts.

The foundation aid districts were largely ignored in the public debates that accompanied the QEA. Nonetheless, we believed that it was important to understand the impact of the major changes wrought by the QEA on this large majority of local districts. Although resource constraints prevented us from including many districts in this category in our case study sample, we did conduct case studies in two foundation aid districts, identified as FN1 and FN2. These districts serve 8,000 and 11,000 students, respectively.

We visited each district several times between 1991 and 1994, collecting budgets and other documents, and interviewing key personnel at the district level and principals, counselors, and teachers in four to eight elementary, middle, and high schools in each district. In addition, all teachers in the sampled schools completed questionnaires twice during the study that addressed conditions in their schools, availability of instructional materials and support, and their curriculum and instructional methods.

The sample of districts included in the case studies was small to permit us to devote the considerable time necessary to develop a detailed understanding of the operations of each district. To complement the case studies and provide more confidence in the findings that emerge from them, we also conducted two surveys of the superintendents of all operating local districts in the state and examined existing state level databases maintained by the SDE on each local district. To capture developments at the state level, we also conducted interviews with key policy makers in the legislature and officials at the SDE.

Together these various strategies of gathering data enabled us to understand the state policy environment that led to the enactment and modification of the QEA; the process of translating the act into actual state policies and procedures; the variation in local contexts that affected the implementation of the act; and the impact of the law on school districts.

OVERVIEW OF THE BOOK

The purpose of this book is to show how school finance reform policies affect the capacity of both rich and poor school districts to serve their students. While our interest is in providing information that is useful to policy makers in a variety of settings, our work is grounded in a particular context—the impact of school finance litigation and legislation in New Jersey. Chapter 2 describes the judicial and state policy context of education in New Jersey, and examines the impact of the QEA on the fiscal equity of the state funding system. Chapter 3 focuses on the demographic, fiscal, and administrative context of the 12 school districts in our study, and on the interaction of state policy and local context. In Chapters 4 through 7, we explore how the capacities of rich and poor school districts changed in the 3 years following the enactment of the QEA, and the reasons for these changes. Chapter 4 focuses on changes in the number and characteristics of education personnel. Chapter 5 explores changes in curriculum and instruction, while Chapter 6 describes developments in social services. The issue of facilities is discussed in Chapter 7. Finally, in Chapter 8 we summarize our findings and discuss policy implications in terms of the educational, financial, and political dimensions.

2

THE STATE CONTEXT
FOR REFORM

A primary objective of school finance reform is to ensure that all children in a state have equal access to a quality education. While school finance laws affect the equity with which dollars are allocated to local school districts, state policies in areas such as education standards, curriculum, assessment, and accountability are intended to influence the scope, content, and excellence of educational programs and services provided students throughout the state. Thus, any discussion of equal educational opportunity must consider the intent, substance, and interaction of both fiscal and nonfiscal education policies.

Education policy in New Jersey has been shaped by 25 years of school finance litigation and by 20 years of state efforts to hold school districts accountable for the way they spend education dollars and the quality of the education they provide their students. This chapter begins with a summary of the two legal challenges to New Jersey's school finance system, *Robinson v Cahill* and *Abbott v Burke*, that have defined the state's constitutional responsibility for elementary and secondary education. The second section examines the major legislative response to the *Abbott* decision, the Quality Education Act (QEA), the resulting allocation of state aid to urban and nonurban school districts, and the impact of this law on the fiscal equity of the state funding system. The third section describes the nonfiscal education policies that provide instructional guidance to schools and school districts, hold school districts accountable for the services they provide, and afford some idea of the state's definition of educational excellence. Throughout the chapter, we show how the court, the legislature, and the state department of education (SDE) have addressed issues of equity, excellence, and efficiency in their actions.

JUDICIAL CONTEXT

A recent review of American states gives New Jersey an A for the adequacy of resources provided for education but a D+ for equity of resource distribution (Education Week, 1997). It is the third wealthiest state in the country after Alaska and Connecticut (National Center for Education Statistics, 1994b), yet the state contains four of the most distressed cities in the United States (Bradbury et al., 1982). While the average cost-adjusted per-pupil expenditure in New Jersey is 48% higher than the national average (National Center for Education Statistics, 1994c), nearly $4,000 per pupil separates high and low spending districts in the state.

These differences are the result of the economic, social, and racial segregation of most of the state's nearly 600 communities. Median household income in the state's two wealthiest counties, Morris and Somerset, for example, is nearly double that of the state's two poorest counties, Cape May and Cumberland. Nearly $31 million per pupil in property wealth separates the state's wealthiest and poorest school districts; the 7:1 difference in per-pupil wealth between Trenton ($150,000) and Princeton ($1,018,000) is typical of the disparities in property wealth across the state. Although 30% of New Jersey's students are members of racial and ethnic minority groups, most African-American and Hispanic students are concentrated in the state's poor urban school districts, leaving New Jersey with the fourth most segregated school system in the country (Orfield, 1994b).

Because of the state's heavy reliance on local property taxes to fund education, these large differences in wealth have translated into large disparities in education spending. In 1989/90, the year prior to the *Abbott* decision, the lowest wealth districts (educating 14% of the state's children) spent $5,017 per pupil on the general education program, while the highest wealth districts (also educating 14% of the state's children) spent, on average, $2,000 per pupil more. Yet, the low wealth districts levied an average school tax rate of $1.21, double that of the highest wealth districts (only $0.60).

This interaction of wealth, spending, and race has sparked years of litigation and two major school finance court cases. The involvement of the courts has affected school finance policy in New Jersey in four ways. First, the state supreme court has established a definition of educational equity and adequacy that is keyed to the educational programs, expenditures, and outcomes of the state's wealthiest communities. Second, the court decisions have driven the agenda for educational finance reform in New Jersey (Lehne, 1978) and provided political cover for two governors who sought to restructure the way the state raises revenues and distributes state aid. Third, in the *Abbott* decision, the court focused attention directly on the plight of poor urban children and the state's responsibility to educate these children. Fourth, the funding laws and state appropriations that resulted from the *Robinson* and *Abbott* decisions ensured that the poorest school districts did not lose ground during the last 20 years. Between 1975/76 and 1993/94, the expenditure level of the lowest spending districts increased from 73% to 76% of the state average, while the school tax rates of the poorest communities dropped nearly $1.00 (Goertz, 1978, 1995).

Robinson v Cahill

The history of school finance litigation in New Jersey began with the filing of the *Robinson v Cahill* case in February 1970. The cities of Jersey City, Paterson, Plainfield, and East Orange joined Kenneth Robinson, a Jersey City student, and his parents in a challenge to the constitutionality of the state's school funding system. The plaintiffs maintained that the system, under which the state provided less than 30% of education revenues, permitted wide variations in per-pupil expenditures from district to district that were related to differences in community wealth. Unlike the situation in other states, cities are among the poorest communities in New Jersey. Because of their limited tax bases, these urban districts were unable to raise as much money for education as their wealthier neighbors, despite higher tax rates.

As a result of this wealth-based spending disparity, the plaintiffs charged, some students received a good education; others were deprived of one that met the state constitutional requirement of a "thorough and efficient" education. This claim was based on Article VIII of the New Jersey Constitution, which calls for the legislature "to provide for the maintenance and support of a thorough and efficient system of free public schools for the instruction of all children in the State between the ages of five and eighteen years." Two issues were central to this and the succeeding litigation: defining a thorough and efficient education, and setting standards against which to measure achievement of the constitutional mandate.

In 1973 the New Jersey Supreme Court ruled that the school funding law violated the "thorough and efficient" clause of the state Constitution. In the first *Robinson* decision, the court defined "thorough and efficient" as that "educational opportunity which is needed in the contemporary setting to equip a child for his role as a citizen and competitor in the labor market" (*Robinson I* at 515) and determined that the constitutional requirement had not been met because of the wide disparities in per-pupil expenditures. The court noted that it used expenditures as a standard because dollar input was plainly relevant and no other viable criterion for measuring compliance with the constitutional mandate had been presented in the case. The court did not mandate expenditure equity, however. It required the state to afford an equal educational opportunity for children, but it allowed districts to spend beyond that required for a thorough and efficient education as long as the excess spending did "not become a device for diluting the State's mandated responsibility" (*Robinson I* at 520 as cited in *Abbott II* at 306).

The Public School Education Act of 1975 (more commonly called Chapter 212) was enacted in response to the *Robinson v Cahill* decision. The law initially increased the state's share of education expenditures from 28% to 40% of total education spending, extending the payment of state aid to districts educating three-quarters of the state's students, and raising total state aid by $400 million. In addition, the statute:

- Defined the major elements of a thorough and efficient education
- Required the state board of education and the commissioner of education to establish statewide education goals and standards and required local districts to set goals, objectives, and standards consistent with statewide goals and objectives
- Established a system for monitoring district compliance with state and local goals and requirements
- Gave the commissioner and the state board of education broad powers to intervene in local fiscal and educational decisions when monitoring revealed deficiencies

The court found the new law facially constitutional in 1976 (*Robinson V*, 1976), but shifted the standard for judging the statute constitutionally adequate from dollar disparities to substantive educational content. While the court recognized the possibility of expenditure disparities under the new funding formula, its primary concern was whether the new finance provisions would "afford sufficient financial support for the system of public education that will emerge from the implementation of the plan set forth in the statute" (*Robinson V* at 464 as cited in *Abbott II* at 309). Money was viewed as only one of a number of elements that give definition and content to the constitutional mandate. Equal expenditures per pupil would be relevant only if it impacted on the substantive education offered in a specific district. "Compliance with the constitutional mandate was to be determined on a district-by-district measurement" (*Abbott II* at 309). The court reserved the right, however, to declare Chapter 212 unconstitutional if, in practice, it did not provide a thorough and efficient education.

Abbott v Burke

The urban school districts challenged the constitutionality of Chapter 212 5 years later. In February 1981, the Education Law Center, a nonprofit public-interest legal organization, filed a complaint in New Jersey Superior Court on behalf of 20 children attending public schools in Camden, East Orange, Irvington, and

Jersey City. The plaintiffs contended that New Jersey's education finance system still caused significant educational expenditure and program disparities between poor urban and wealthy suburban school districts, leaving poor urban districts unable to meet the educational needs of their students. They argued that the operation of Chapter 212 violated both the "thorough and efficient" and the equal protection clauses of the state Constitution and the Law Against Discrimination. The state responded that disparities resulted instead from inadequate effort and mismanagement by local school districts. It argued that the level and mechanism for distributing state aid were adequate and that the state's system of monitoring school districts was sufficient to ensure the provision of a thorough and efficient education.

Arguments before the courts focused initially on procedural issues. In 1985 the New Jersey Supreme Court finally remanded the case, *Abbott v Burke*, to the Office of Administrative Law (OAL) for the development of a complete record (*Abbott I*, 1985). After a hearing that lasted 9 months, OAL Judge Lefelt ruled in August 1988 that Chapter 212 failed to provide a thorough and efficient education because educational opportunity in New Jersey continued to be determined by community wealth (*Abbott v Burke*, 1988). On June 5, 1990, the supreme court concurred with Judge Lefelt and ruled that Chapter 212 was unconstitutional as applied to poorer urban districts because the education delivered to the students was neither thorough nor efficient (*Abbott II*). The justices found that

> under the present system . . . the poorer the district and the greater its need, the less the money available, and the worse the education. . . . Education has failed there, for both the student and the State. (*Abbott II* at 295)

In these two *Abbott* decisions, the court expanded the constitutional standard for a thorough and efficient education to one that assures *disadvantaged students* the opportunity to compete in, and contribute to, the society entered by their *relatively advantaged peers*. "Thorough and efficient means more than teaching the skills needed to compete in the labor market" (*Abbott II* at 363), the definition the court had established in *Robinson I*. It means the ability to fulfill one's role as a citizen; to participate fully in society, in the life of one's community; to appreciate music, art, and literature, and to share that with friends. The justices wrote:

> We have decided this case on the premise that the children of poorer urban districts are as capable as all others; that their deficiencies stem from their socioeconomic status; and that through effective education and changes in that socioeconomic status, they can perform as well as others. Our constitutional mandate does not allow us to consign poorer children permanently to an inferior education on the theory that they cannot afford a better one or that they would not benefit from it. (*Abbott II* at 340)

The court then determined that the constitutional mandate of a thorough and efficient education had not been satisfied in poorer urban districts. It based its conclusion on both the absolute level of education in those districts and on the comparison of educational programs in science, foreign language, computers, music and art, industrial arts, and physical education with those in affluent suburban districts:

> Science education is deficient in some poorer urban districts. Princeton has seven laboratories in its high school, each with built-in equipment.... However, many poorer districts offer science classes in labs built in the 1920's and 1930's, where sinks do not work, equipment such as microscopes is not available, supplies for chemistry or biology classes are insufficient, and hands-on investigative techniques cannot be taught. (at 360)

> The disparity in foreign-language programs is dramatic. Montclair's students begin instruction in French or Spanish at the pre-school level. In Princeton's middle school, fifth grade students must take a half-year of French and a half-year of Spanish.... Jersey City starts its foreign language program in the ninth grade; Paterson begins it at the tenth grade. (at 360)

> Music programs are vastly superior in some richer suburban districts. South Brunswick offers music classes starting in kindergarten.... Princeton offers several performing groups, including bands, choruses, and small ensembles.... However, Camden and Paterson do not offer a music course until the fourth grade; only introductory level music courses are offered in the high school. In 1981, Camden eliminated all its elementary school music teachers and provided "helpers" to assist in teaching music. (at 361)

> Physical education programs in some poorer urban districts are deficient.... In East Orange High School ... the track team practices in the second floor hallway. All of Irvington's elementary schools have no outdoor play space; some of the playgrounds had been converted to faculty parking lots. (at 362)

The state contended that students in poorer urban districts need intensive training in basic skills first; that these students cannot now benefit from the superior range of course offerings found in the wealthier districts. The court responded, however, that the result violated not only its sense of what constitutes a thorough and efficient education, but Chapter 212 as well, which requires a "breadth of program offerings designed to develop the individual talents and abilities of students" (at 365).

The court looked beyond the educational program to disparities in personnel, facilities, and the educational needs of students. It found that most schools in richer suburban districts were newer, cleaner, and safer than those in poorer urban districts. The schools in the poor urban communities were old, crumbling, and lacked adequate instructional space. Teacher ratios, experience, and education were greater in districts with high property wealth, per-pupil expenditure, and socioeconomic status. Students from poorer urban districts were considerably less likely to pass the state's basic skills tests and considerably more likely to drop out of school than their peers in wealthy suburban communities. The court wrote that the needs of poor urban children go beyond education to include the needs that arise in communities characterized by violence, poverty and despair. As a result, students in poorer urban districts require *more* resources than students in wealthy communities.

The court also held that state aid under Chapter 212 that is counter-equalizing—that increases funding disparities and that has no arguable educational or administrative justification—was unconstitutional. It found the minimum aid provision of Chapter 212 unconstitutional because "its sole function is to enable richer districts to spend even more, thereby increasing the disparity of educational funding between richer and poorer" (at 382). The court did not consider categorical aid and transportation aid counter-equalizing because the funds go to all districts and the programs have clear educational purposes: to help offset the cost of educating students with special educational needs and of transporting students, regardless of where they reside.

The court ordered the legislature to design a new or revised funding system that would meet the following criteria:

1. *Equalize spending for the regular education program between poorer urban districts and property-rich districts.* The court defined "poorer urban districts" as those 28 districts that were classified by the department of education as "urban districts" *and* fell within District Factor Groups (DFG) A and B. These districts educated about 25% of the state's students. The DFGs were derived from a composite measure of community social and economic variables, such as educational and occupational background of the population, per-capita income of the district, and mobility. Districts were ranked from low to high on this measure and divided into ten approximately equal groups. The DFGs ranged from A (lowest socioeconomic status districts) to J (highest socioeconomic status districts) (*Abbott II* at 342, fn. 18). The court defined "property-rich districts" as those 108 districts in DFGs I and J, the two highest socioeconomic status groups. If the state allowed the richer suburban districts to increase their spending, it must increase the funding of the poorer urban districts accordingly.

2. *Provide additional funds to meet the special education needs of the urban districts in order to redress their disadvantages.* Such assistance must be in addition to the funds needed to redress disparities in the regular education programs.

3. *Assure that funding for poor urban districts is certain every year and does not depend on the budgeting or taxing decisions of local school boards.* The legislature could not meet the constitutional mandate simply by raising the guaranteed tax base under Chapter 212. The design of the funding plan was supposed to take into consideration the municipal overburden of the poorer urban districts.
4. *Eliminate minimum aid.*
5. *Implement a new formula starting in the 1991/92 school year.* The new system would be phased in. If the legislature provided for a phase-in of the new funding plan, minimum aid could be phased out in accordance with that timetable.

The *Abbott* decision applied only to poorer urban districts. The justices ruled that sufficient evidence was not submitted in this case to show that the constitutional mandate was violated in other school districts in the state.

FISCAL POLICY CONTEXT

On July 3, 1990, one month after the *Abbott v Burke* decision, Governor Jim Florio signed into law a new school funding formula, the Quality Education Act of 1990. At the time of its passage, the QEA was heralded as a major step toward the reform of urban education and the achievement of school finance equity in New Jersey. Yet, as described in Chapter 1, over the next 9 months the law was assaulted by citizens and major education interest groups throughout the state. In March 1991, four months before the QEA was to take effect, it was amended to provide greater property tax relief to taxpayers and less aid to the financially strapped urban school districts.

The Quality Education Act

State education aid programs can serve many purposes. The primary role of state aid is to offset disparities in education expenditures caused by variations in local wealth. This is the traditional definition of "equalization." Equalization formulas, in turn, can focus on *student equity* (assuring that all students receive an equal level of educational resources) or on *taxpayer equity* (assuring that school districts that make the same tax effort for education receive equal resources). State aid can also be used to compensate for expenditure differences related to student need (e.g., the extra cost of educating students with disabilities, limited English proficiency, and so forth) or district need (e.g., the higher costs of providing services in urban school districts or isolated rural districts). Finally, state aid formulas can be designed to encourage the efficient use of public dollars by including provisions such as expenditure caps or penalties for excessive spending on functions like administration.

The QEA was designed to increase the equity of the state's funding system, while establishing a floor of fiscal support for an adequate educational program through its foundation aid program. The higher costs of special needs students are addressed through categorical aid programs. Other elements of the formula, like state and local budget caps, were intended to promote the efficient use of educational dollars at both levels of government.

FOUNDATION AID FORMULA

Under the QEA, the state allocated aid for the "regular program" through a foundation aid formula. This approach guarantees that every student's education is supported, at a minimum, by a state-defined level of expenditure, or foundation, regardless of the wealth of the local community. Local school districts must contribute to this amount, typically by applying a state-established tax rate to a district's wealth. State aid is the difference between the foundation amount and the district's required contribution. Therefore, districts with greater per-pupil wealth will have a larger local contribution and will receive less state aid than those districts with less wealth.

For 1992/93, the QEA established a base foundation of $6,742 per pupil enrolled in a regular program in grades 1 through 5. The drafters of the original QEA had set the foundation amount for 1991/92 at $6,835, about the 60th percentile of spending. This was an amount they considered generally sufficient for districts to provide an adequate educational program, but this level was reduced when the QEA was amended. The foundation amount included the cost of teacher pensions and social security because the original version of the QEA transferred these costs from the state to the local school district. This provision was never implemented, but the foundation amount was not adjusted downward accordingly. Instead, each district's maximum foundation budget was reduced by the amount of state pension and social security aid paid on behalf of a district's resident students.

All pupils were assigned grade-level or program weights that essentially reflected expected differences in class sizes and course offerings, especially in the upper grades. For example, students in grades 1 through 5 were counted as 1.0, those in grades 6 through 8 were weighted at 1.1, and students in high school were weighted 1.33. Each district's maximum foundation budget was then calculated by multiplying the base foundation amount by the total number of weighted pupils. Also included in the maximum foundation budget was an additional $113 per unweighted pupil to maintain school facilities. The facilities foundation replaced aid for capital outlay, which also was wealth equalized under the prior law. Facilities aid could be "banked" in a capital reserve fund or used for ongoing maintenance activities.

Under orders from the court to equalize spending in poorer urban districts, the QEA defined a category of *special needs* districts. A district was determined to be a special needs district if it met the court definition of a poorer urban district, or if 15% of its students were eligible for Aid to Families with Dependent Children and at least 1,000 such students were enrolled in the district. This second criterion, which was added in the legislation, increased the number of special needs districts to 30. The QEA raised the base foundation for special needs districts by 5%.

The state calculated a district's required contribution, or in the QEA language, "local fair share," based on its property wealth and aggregate personal income. Income was a new component in the wealth measure under the QEA and was added to address the concern that the personal incomes of residents from middle-income suburban communities (as well as shore communities and some developing rural areas) had not kept pace with rapidly escalating property values in the 1980s. Each district's local fair share was calculated by applying a statewide property tax rate, or multiplier, to its equalized property value and a statewide income tax rate, or multiplier, to its personal income, and dividing the sum of these two products by two. Special needs districts had their local fair share calculated using only an adjusted property tax multiplier if this resulted in a lower amount. A district's state foundation aid was the difference between its maximum foundation budget (adjusted for teacher pension and social security costs) and its local fair share, with a deduction for excess surplus.

Most districts were not mandated to spend at the level of the maximum foundation budget or tax up to the local fair share amount determined by the state. This was a concession to districts in southern New Jersey, which generally spend less on education than the rest of the state. Non–special needs districts would receive their full foundation aid entitlement regardless of their spending and taxing decisions. Special needs districts could levy the lesser of their 1990/91 school tax levy or their local fair share. Districts could also spend above the foundation level, but this extra spending did not generate any additional state aid. The extent of local leeway was constrained only by budget caps.

TRANSITION AID

Abbott II declared minimum aid unconstitutional, but permitted a phase-out of this aid. Transition aid was the mechanism in the QEA for phasing out minimum aid. This aid, which was supposed to be phased out at a rate of 25% a year for four years, made up the difference between 106.5% of a district's 1990/91 base state aid (foundation aid plus categorical aid) and its 1991/92 year aid.

CATEGORICAL AID

New Jersey continued to use categorical aid programs that were not wealth-equalized to provide additional resources for students needing services in special education, bilingual education, and vocational education, and for "at-risk" students. (The supreme court upheld this approach in *Abbott II* because of educational policy considerations.) Weights reflecting the cost of educating students with different education needs were multiplied by the number of students served in the program and a foundation amount for categorical programs that was $7,232 in 1992/93. The state had programmatic mandates in special education, bilingual education, and compensatory education.

The QEA replaced the former compensatory education program with aid for pupils *at risk of educational failure*. Aid payments were based upon the number of public school pupils eligible for the federal free lunch or free milk program; eligibility thus reflected household income. The at-risk student weight was 0.151 times the student's grade-level weight. Districts could use aid for compensatory education programs or for any other services or programs that addressed the needs of at-risk pupils. Districts were still required to provide remedial services to students who did not meet state-established standards.

DISTRICT AND STATE EXPENDITURE CAPS

The QEA continued to cap increases in a district's total current expense and capital outlay budgets as a way of encouraging more efficient use of education dollars, and of equalizing spending. Allowable growth in education spending was tied to the 3-year average change in per-capita income and the ratio of each district's actual budget to its maximum foundation budget. Non–special needs districts were limited to a 5.6% to 6.75% increase in 1992/93.

A separate "equity spending" cap was calculated for each special needs district. In this case, the rate of growth was determined by how far each district was from projected parity in 1995/96. Caps on the special needs districts ranged from 6% to 22% in 1992/93. The equity spending caps, coupled with the 5% extra weight in the foundation base, were intended to bring about the court-mandated spending parity between the special needs and wealthy districts.

A district could exceed its cap only if it received a cap waiver from the commissioner of education or from its voters. The QEA limited the circumstances under which cap waivers could be given by the commissioner to districts experiencing increases in enrollment (exceeding 2%) and in special education costs (exceeding 5%), with specified lease purchase agreements, or those that have tuition agreements with special services districts. Voters could approve a cap waiver for any other reason with a majority vote.

The QEA also limited increases in total state education aid ("maximum school aid"), a category that included foundation aid, teacher retirement costs, and categorical aid programs (except debt service), and represented over 90% of total state aid to education. In general, aid increases were limited to the 3-year average growth in per-capita income plus one percentage point (to allow for increases in enrollments and changes in categorical program weights). In 1992/93, growth was limited to 80% of this rate.

The Impact of Changes in State Aid.

Between 1990/91 and 1993/94, the years covered by our study, state aid increased by $885 million, or 25%, as shown in Table 2.1. Aid for the "regular education" program—foundation aid—increased $814.4 million, and aid for categorical programs—special education, bilingual education, at-risk aid, and transportation aid—grew another $457.1 million. These increases were offset by a *reduction* in teacher retirement costs of $415 million due to the revaluation of teacher pensions.

About half (51.3%) of these new aid dollars were allocated to the 30 special needs districts in the state. This level of allocation is only a modest change, as the special needs districts received 42% of state aid for current and capital expenditures the year prior to the QEA. In dollar terms, this group of districts received an additional $652.7 million in aid in the 3-year period 1990/91 to 1993/94, a 61.3% increase over 1990/91 as shown in Table 2.2. Although the QEA began to phase out minimum aid, the high wealth districts lost less than $3 million in general aid between 1990 and 1993. This reduction was more than offset by a large increase in special education aid and increases in other categorical aid programs. As a result, these districts realized a $35.6 million, or 20%, increase in state aid under the QEA. Foundation aid districts received an additional $583 million in aid, a 45% increase over 1990.

This large infusion of aid had a minimal impact on the equity of New Jersey's funding system, however. Between 1989/90 (the year prior to the *Abbott* decision) and 1993/94, the difference between expenditures at the 5th and 95th percentiles remained unchanged at nearly $4,000 per pupil. The correlation between the property wealth of the state's districts and their expenditures of 0.43 also stayed the same during this period. These are summary equity mea-

TABLE 2.1. *State education aid, 1990/91 and 1993/94 (in millions)*

CATEGORY	1990/91	1993/94	$ CHANGE	% CHANGE
Foundation Aid[a]	$1808.7	$2623.1	$814.4	45.0
Teacher Retirement	925.4	510.2	−415.2	−44.9
Special Education Aid	347.3	582.5	235.2	67.7
Bilingual Education Aid	41.6	57.4	15.8	38.0
At-Risk Aid[b]	150.5	293.0	142.5	94.7
Transportation Aid	200.2	263.8	63.6	31.8
TOTAL	$3473.7	$4358.7[c]	$885.0	25.5

[a]For 1990–91, includes equalization aid, minimum aid and local vocational aid, but not capital outlay aid. For 1993–94, includes transition aid and facilities aid.
[b]Distributed as compensatory education aid in 1990–91
[c]Includes county vocational aid.

TABLE 2.2. *State education aid by district type, 1990/91 and 1993/94 (in millions)*

CATEGORY	SPECIAL NEEDS DISTRICTS		FOUNDATION AID DISTRICTS		TRANSITION AID DISTRICTS	
	$ CHANGE	% CHANGE	$ CHANGE	% CHANGE	$ CHANGE	% CHANGE
Foundation aid[a]	$458.5	51.8%	$358.3	42.6%	–$2.4	–2.9%
Special education aid	66.0	79.8	139.9	62.8	29.3	69.8
Bilingual aid	7.7	27.5	6.4	58.7	1.7	63.0
At-risk aid[b]	104.0	131.0	37.2	59.8	1.3	14.6
Transportation aid	16.5	54.8	41.3	30.7	5.8	16.3
Total	$652.7	61.3	$583.1	44.5%	$35.6	20.5%

[a] For 1990–91, includes equalization aid, minimum aid and local vocational aid, but not capital outlay aid. For 1993–94, includes transition aid and facilities aid.
[b] Distributed as compensatory education aid in 1990–91.

sures, however, and may obscure changes that took place among districts within the state.

Table 2.3 divides the state's districts into seven groups (septiles) based on the property wealth of the district. The septiles, which have approximately the same number of students, are ranked from low wealth (septile 1) to high wealth (septile 7). This septile analysis confirms the findings that the first 3 years of the QEA did little to reduce inequities in spending. In 1993/94, more than $1,500 per pupil still separated the lowest and highest wealth septiles. Tax rate differences had narrowed, however. While the average tax rate in Septile 1 remained the same, tax rates in the wealthier communities rose considerably. As a result, the amount of money the poor districts could raise per $1.00 of tax rate for the regular education program (net current expenditures or NCE per pupil) rose from 36% to 57% of the high wealth communities—$5,826 versus $10,164.

This analysis also shows that the equalizing impact of the QEA was concentrated in the lowest spending districts. Between 1989/90 and 1993/94, the two lowest wealth groups substantially increased the dollars they could raise per $1.00 of school tax rate (40% in Septile 1 and 20% in Septile 2), while the "rate of return" fell in the higher wealth groups.

TABLE 2.3. *Changes in net current expense per pupil and school tax rates, 1989/90 to 1993/94*
(districts grouped by property wealth per pupil)

Wealth Septile	1989/1990			1993/1994			Change, 1989/1993	
	Net Current Expense/Pupil	School Tax Rate	NCE/$1.00 of School Taxes	Net Current Expense/Pupil	School Tax Rate	NCE/$1.00 of School Taxes	Net Current Expense/Pupil	School Tax Rate
1	$5017	1.21	$4171	$6991	1.20	$5826	$1974	-0.01
2	4656	1.02	4458	6159	1.15	5356	1503	+0.13
3	5214	1.02	5111	6489	1.33	4879	1275	+0.31
4	5424	1.02	5317	6867	1.31	5242	1443	+0.29
5	5664	0.98	5625	7015	1.34	5253	1351	+0.36
6	6353	0.89	7028	7646	1.23	6216	1293	+0.34
7	7025	0.60	11513	8538	0.84	10164	1513	+0.24

Tax rates in the middle wealth communities also rose rapidly, and by 1993/94, often exceeded the tax rates of low wealth communities. As a result, the number of dollars that middle income communities received per $1.00 of tax effort were *less than* those raised in the lowest wealth communities. What contributed to the changing status of the middle wealth communities in New Jersey? There are several factors at play. First, these communities increased their aggregate spending by about 35% between 1990/91 and 1993/94 to address growing enrollments, fixed costs, and salary settlements. Second, these increases in education expenditures greatly outstripped growth in state aid. While school spending on the regular education program increased an average of $1,350 per pupil in Septiles 3 through 5, state equalization aid increased only $405 per pupil. In this 3-year period, state aid as a percentage of spending on the *regular* education program remained constant at about 27% for these districts, while the state share of all current and capital expenditures was closer to 35%. Thus, middle wealth districts had to increase their local taxes considerably to fund spending growth. Finally, the tax bases of middle income districts grew too slowly—less than 1% a year—to support these increased revenue demands. When adjusted for enrollment changes, the average per-pupil valuation *dropped* nearly 6% in the three groups of middle wealth districts. This drove school tax rates up even higher.

The New Jersey Supreme Court required the state to achieve "substantial" spending equity between the state's special needs and wealthy districts. Expenditure parity was evaluated by comparing per-pupil expenditures for the regular education program in each of the 30 special needs districts with the average expenditure of the state's wealthiest school districts—those in District Factor Groups I and J. Figure 2.1 shows that, *on average*, the expenditure disparity decreased from $1,714 per pupil to $1,295 per pupil between 1989/90 and 1993/94. When we look at individual district data, in 1989/90 disparities ranged from $582 to $3,647, and exceeded $2,000 per pupil in thirteen districts. By 1993/94, disparities ranged from $160 to $2,165, and one district spent $895 per pupil more than the I and J average. Spending differences had *widened*, however, in six of the 30 special needs districts, and disparities still exceeded $2,000 in six of the districts.

Challenges to the QEA

The failure of the QEA to narrow significantly the spending disparities between the special needs and wealthy suburban districts, and the realization that the mechanics of the law would prevent the court-mandated equalization, sent the *Abbott* plaintiffs back into court. They charged that the QEA, as applied, failed to assure that:

FIGURE 2.1. *Mean per-pupil expenditures for special needs districts and transition aid districts in 1990 and 1993*

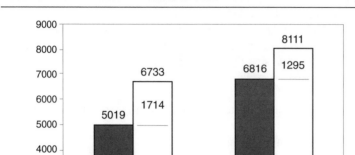

1. Spending on the regular education program would become substantially equal between the special needs and the more affluent districts
2. Adequate funds would be provided to address the special educational needs of students in special needs districts
3. Funding would be certain and not dependent on local taxing and budgeting decisions
4. Municipal overburden would be considered

They, therefore, asked the court to declare the QEA unconstitutional. In a per curiam decision issued in July 1994, the court reaffirmed its prior holding in *Abbott II* and found the QEA unconstitutional because it failed to assure parity of regular education expenditures between the special needs districts and the more affluent districts (*Abbott v Burke*, 136 N.J. 444). The court ordered the state to adopt a new funding formula by September 1996 that would assure substantial parity, "approximating 100%," and provide for special education needs for the 1997/98 school year. It also charged the state to address the existing disparity in the upcoming school years of 1995/96 and 1996/97. The court retained jurisdiction over the case and agreed to entertain applications for relief if the state did not meet the court's timetable.

Meanwhile, the interaction of different provisions of the QEA began to cause problems for the middle wealth districts as well. In 1992/93, growth in the teacher retirement and categorical aid programs outstripped the permitted increase in maximum school aid. As a result, in the initial 1992/93 QEA budget, foundation aid was *reduced* by $34 million. The decision to revalue all state pension funds, including the teacher pension fund, lowered pension contributions for 1992/93 by $342 million, freeing up these dollars for foundation aid. This revaluation, however, was a "one-shot" adjustment.

The threat of aid cuts to middle-income suburban districts in 1992/93 triggered several actions. First, the foundation aid districts began calling for changes to the QEA. Second, suburban Republican legislators introduced a constitutional amendment in June 1992 that would have replaced the current "thorough and efficient" clause with a funding formula that would limit the state's financial obligation to all school districts and would eliminate the requirement of substantial parity between poor urban and wealthy suburban districts. This full-scale retreat from the long-held constitutional mandate of the state's obligation to provide a quality education to all children was opposed by all the major education and advocacy groups. The Republicans dropped their plan to put the amendment on the November 1992 ballot, but subsequently introduced a new funding law that incorporated many of the provisions of the proposed constitutional amendment.

In response to the threat of the constitutional amendment and Republican funding plan, the major education groups (who are members of the New Jersey Association for Public Schools[NJAPS]); groups representing urban districts, foundation aid districts, and wealthier suburban districts; and the Education Law Center proposed a compromise plan for the 1993/94 school year. This plan, which was enacted by the legislature in December 1992 as the Public School Reform Act of 1992, provided incremental increases in foundation aid (9% to the special needs districts and 4% to the non–special needs districts), froze categorical aid (special education, at-risk, and bilingual education aid) at 1992/93 levels for each district, and ensured that transition aid districts received no less aid than they received in 1992/93.

In the absence of further legislation, funding under the QEA was to have been resumed in 1994/95. In face of the court decision, the QEA was not resurrected and, through footnote language in the state's budget, the legislature essentially froze state aid for the 1994/95 school year. The state redistributed $29 million of transition aid from the high wealth to the special needs districts, but no other increases were provided.

THE BROADER EDUCATION POLICY CONTEXT

School finance has dominated education policy discussions and decisions for the last two decades in New Jersey. The state has developed a number of other education policies, however, that are designed to provide instructional guidance to schools and school districts and to hold these entities accountable for the provision of educational services and the performance of their students.

Instructional Guidance

Governments use an array of policies to guide classroom work: curriculum frameworks, assessment of student performance, instructional materials, oversight of instruction, or requirements for teacher education and licensure (Cohen and Spillane, 1993). Since the passage of the Public School Education Act of 1975, curricular change has been driven by the state's assessment system. State policy makers assumed that as the state made the test more difficult (and expanded the subject areas covered), district instructional practices would change to meet the new testing standards. The Whitman administration is taking a more systemic approach to education reform, starting with curriculum content standards that will drive the development of state curriculum frameworks and state assessments. At the time of our study, however, the primary instrument of reform was the state testing program. In addition, the state developed a small technical assistance program targeted at the special needs of the urban school districts.

STUDENT TESTING

New Jersey uses statewide assessments to monitor school district progress, identify students in need of compensatory education services, and hold both students and school districts accountable for their performance. Students in grades 3, 6, and 9, or 11 have been assessed in reading and mathematics since 1978. In 1976, the legislature enacted a Minimum Basic Skills (MBS) test as part of a compromise to gain support for the state income tax needed to fund the state's school finance law. Urban interests supported this provision as a means of holding urban school systems accountable to the education of disadvantaged children (Goertz & Hannigan, 1978). Legislation enacted in 1979 made passage of the ninth grade test a requirement for receiving a high school diploma. Results from the MBS were used in all three grades to identify students in need of remedial assistance and to generate state compensatory education aid payments. Scores were reported publicly on a district-by-district basis and were a major component of the state's monitoring system.

The high stakes nature of the MBS test led districts to align their curriculum to the tested skills and led teachers to focus their instruction on these skills. By 1982, scores on the MBS had improved dramatically, and most students had a firm mastery of the basic skills. State policy makers saw a need to expand the focus of the state assessment program beyond basic skills to encompass the more rigorous knowledge and skills that students would need to function "socially, politically and economically in a democratic society" (Koffler, 1987).

The state implemented a new statewide testing system in 1983. The third and sixth grade MBS tests were replaced by commercial tests chosen by each district. The SDE compared the commercial tests to the high school graduation test, and established proficiency standards for each of the major tests. These standards are used for school and district accountability and for identifying students in need of remedial services. The ninth grade MBS test was replaced with a more rigorous High School Proficiency Test (HSPT), and the subject areas were expanded to include writing as well as reading and mathematics.

In 1988, the legislature voted to move the high school graduation test from 9th to 11th grade. Like the 9th grade HSPT, the new test requires students to apply basic skills in complex ways, such as interpreting reading passages, solving multistep problems, and writing coherent essays—but at a more advanced level. The new HSPT also uses more alternative test formats than the older test, which was predominantly multiple choice. The state also implemented an Early Warning Test (EWT) in 8th grade to identify students at risk of not passing the HSPT. The new HSPT applied first to the graduating class of 1995; it was given to 11th grade students in fall of 1993.

TECHNICAL ASSISTANCE

The QEA was designed to target additional funds to the state's urban districts. At the same time, the SDE undertook several initiatives to improve the scope and quality of education programs in these communities. These activities included the provision of technical assistance by a newly created Division of Urban Education (DUE) and the establishment of programs linking education and social services.

The DUE was established initially to assist the 30 special needs districts to develop and implement Education Improvement Plans (EIP), a requirement for spending new dollars generated by the QEA. The DUE saw its mission as going beyond monitoring compliance with the EIPs, however, to one of stimulating urban education reform. The goals of the division, which was in operation between 1991 and 1993, included promoting organizational change in urban schools and urban school districts; fostering an integrated system of educational and social services to urban schools and families; promoting professional growth and renewal in urban schools; and identifying, generating, and linking resources to the needs of urban schools.

Among the programs supported by the DUE was Dr. James Comer's school improvement program. The Comer model stresses parent involvement, the sharing of authority by educators, and the regular use of guidance and mental health counselors to solve behavioral problems (Comer, 1996). Three

SDE employees received training in the Comer model and supported the implementation of the program in 31 schools in 16 special needs districts. The SDE also introduced Robert Slavin's Success for All program (Slavin, 1990) and Henry Levin's Accelerated Schools model (Levin, 1987) in 7 special needs schools. In addition, the SDE worked with the department of human services to facilitate the implementation and maintenance of pilot school-based youth services programs in 13 of the urban districts.

CURRICULUM CONTENT STANDARDS

While assessment has been the primary instrument of education change in New Jersey for nearly 20 years, the state recently enacted curriculum content standards that identify what all students should know and be able to do. A new monitoring law, enacted by the legislature in 1991, called for the establishment of standards in grades K through 4, 5 through 8, and 9 through 12 in eight subject areas: language arts/literacy, mathematics, science, social studies, world languages, the arts, health/physical education, and career education. Committees developed draft standards in 1992/93, but their work was held in abeyance during subsequent changes in the leadership of the SDE. The draft standards were reviewed and revised in 1995, and were approved by the State Board of Education in May 1996. The SDE is developing a new statewide fourth grade assessment aligned with the new standards, and the department plans to revise the EWT and HSPT to reflect the more rigorous content standards.

Accountability

From the initial development of the QEA, the governor's office and legislature were concerned about how school districts that received large increases in state aid, especially urban communities, would use their funds. Governor Florio (1990) made the avoidance of waste an important part of his defense of spending increases:

> Let me make it very, very clear what this money is not for: It's not for anyone to build up flabby, lethargic bureaucracies. It's not for empire-building by administrators. It's not for business as usual in systems that have been producing poor results. [It's] not for anyone's patronage. [It's] not for anyone's personal agenda. It's for one thing and one thing only: our children. . . . Education today will be more than the three "R's." It also needs a "Big A": accountability. (p. 79)

This thinking led the legislature and SDE to enact a set of fiscal, planning, program-targeting, and monitoring regulations to guide and control how the urban districts spent their new funds.

First, as discussed above, the legislature limited how much a district could increase its spending through a series of budget caps. In most of the urban districts, increases in state aid in the first year of the QEA were greater than permitted increases in spending, forcing the special needs districts to use $82 million of their new state aid for property tax relief.

Second, each special needs district was required to develop and submit an annual EIP to the commissioner of education that identified educational goals for each district, strategies for achieving these goals, and how new QEA dollars would be used to implement the strategies. The EIPs were to incorporate the recommendations of "external review teams" (ERT) of state employees, local educators, and representatives of social service providers and advocacy groups who examined the educational programs, governance, management, and finance of the special needs districts in the fall of 1990. The EIPs had to be approved by the commissioner of education, who under the QEA, had to assure that the local districts' budgets provided the resources necessary to implement the approved plan, including necessary technical support. In the second year of the QEA, the state required that EIPs focus much more explicitly on student outcomes and that the EIP expenditures be tied more closely to these outcomes.

Third, the state initiated a program-targeting requirement in the second year of the EIPs. The initial version of the QEA had included a provision that required districts whose foundation budgets increased by more than 10% to submit a plan to the department of education for the use of this additional aid. These plans were to incorporate "policies and programs whose educational effectiveness has been demonstrated." The commissioner of education was supposed to identify educationally effective programs to guide the districts in the development of these educational improvement plans. The department did not develop a list of effective programs, and the targeting provision was dropped when the QEA was amended in 1991. In the fall of 1992, however, the SDE incorporated program targeting into the revised EIP regulations. Each school was to generate a school improvement plan (SIP) based on what it determined as "demonstrably effective programs" for improving student achievement. A list of these programs was to be prepared by the DUE, and each special needs district was to allocate $50 per student to each school to support the SIPs.

Fourth, the special needs districts underwent two levels of monitoring. To ensure implementation of the EIP plans, each district was assigned a representative from the DUE. The district liaison made a monthly verification visit to each special needs district to review the status of completed EIP objectives, verify EIP expenditures to date, conduct site visits to schools, and identify needs for technical assistance or concerns regarding any aspect of implementation.

While the DUE monitored compliance with the EIP, many of the special needs districts also had to meet the requirements of the state's statewide education monitoring system. This system, which was initially developed under

Chapter 212 and overhauled in 1984, defined education standards through 43 indicators grouped into 10 categories, including comprehensive curriculum/instruction, student attendance, facilities, affirmative action, finance, and school community relations. One of the most important indicators was achievement on state tests. Seventy-five percent of third, sixth, and ninth graders in each school in a district had to meet the state minimum proficiency standards in reading, mathematics, and writing (high school only). The county superintendents monitored districts by conducting desk audits and on-site school evaluation visits. If after this "Level I monitoring" a district satisfied all 10 criteria, it was certified for 5 years. Those that did not pass Level I monitoring went through two increasingly rigorous remediation steps ("Level II" and "Level III" monitoring). Districts that did not pass Level III monitoring could face state takeover.

At the time the QEA was enacted, one-third of the 30 special needs districts were in Level II monitoring, and a number were in Level III monitoring. With the passage of the new monitoring law, the SDE suspended Level I monitoring until the 1993/94 school year, while a new system was designed and piloted. The state continued to monitor those districts in Level II and Level III, however, for compliance with the old regulations.

SUMMARY

Twenty-five years of litigation, legislation, and regulation have established the parameters of an equitable, adequate, and efficient elementary and secondary education system in New Jersey. The New Jersey Supreme Court has defined an adequate education as one that prepares all students to fulfill their roles as citizens, to participate fully in society and in the life of their community, and to appreciate music, art, and literature. The court's standard for such an adequate education is the educational program afforded students in the state's wealthiest communities. Thus, under the court mandate, equality of educational opportunity requires the state to equalize expenditures for the regular program between the poorest and wealthiest school districts. The state must provide additional resources to address the special needs of students in the poor districts.

While the court focused on expenditure equalization as a way of increasing educational opportunities for poor students, the legislature and SDE turned to other policies to drive changes in curriculum and instruction in low performing school districts. The state assessment system embodied increasingly higher standards in a limited number of subject areas—reading, writing, and mathematics. The accountability system ensured that low performing students, schools, and school districts paid attention to these standards, and a small program of technical assistance helped some schools and districts identify appropriate educational interventions.

The legislature began to address the court's decision through its QEA. The designers of the original law set the original foundation level at an amount they felt was sufficient to provide an adequate education. Increases in categorical funds for at-risk students and students with disabilities were intended to provide additional services to special needs students. However, a political backlash against the large increase in state taxes required to fund the new law, and concerns about the potential cost of the new law and potential misuse of the new state aid dollars led to the enactment of provisions limiting the growth in state education aid, as well as in education spending in low- and moderate-wealth communities. The interaction of these and other elements of the QEA limited the equalizing impact of the law. After two years and an infusion of nearly a billion dollars, the overall equity of the system remained substantially unchanged, and large disparities remained between many of the state's poor urban and wealthy suburban communities.

The capacity of state fiscal and other education policies to ensure that all students in New Jersey have access to a "thorough and efficient" education as defined by the court is contingent on several factors. First, how rigorous are the educational standards embodied in these policies? Years of minimum basic skills testing combined with state monitoring and increased resources improved the basic skills of students in New Jersey. But the court has made it clear that a focus on low-level skills falls short of preparing all students to be competitive workers and productive members of society. The new content standards enacted by the state board of education are said to be rigorous and to embody national academic standards. The extent to which they are implemented across the state will be determined by their integration into the state's assessment, accountability, and school finance systems, and the capacity of school districts to respond to them.

Second, are these policies designed to enhance the capacity of school districts to support the new standards? As discussed in Chapters 4 through 7, these capacities include well-trained personnel, appropriate curriculum and instruction, and quality facilities and student-support services. What will it cost to enhance these capacities? To what extent will this require additional dollars, and to what extent can school districts reasonably be expected to use existing funds more efficiently? What kinds of technical support are needed?

Third, how does state policy interact with community context and the local policy context? Although state leaders can set in motion a variety of fiscal and other education policies, these policies unfold within the hundreds of local school districts located in diverse local communities and policy contexts. These various local forces shape and reshape the actual implementation of state policies in ways that cannot always be anticipated at the state level. This is the focus of the next chapter.

3

INEQUITIES IN THE LOCAL CONTEXTS FOR EDUCATION

A s states have become more active in generating educational policies, it has become increasingly clear that the effects of state actions are mediated in complex ways by local contexts (Fuhrman, Clune, & Elmore, 1988; Fullan, 1991). It is important to understand the different ways in which school districts interpret and enact intendedly evenhanded policies. Moreover, in the case of finance policy, it is essential to understand the differences in the needs of the communities and student populations that school resources must address.

To develop an understanding of how our sample of local districts in New Jersey responded to the fiscal and nonfiscal provisions of the Quality Education Act (QEA) and other state policies, we examine three important dimensions of the local context for reform. First, we discuss the characteristics of the communities and student populations served by these twelve districts. We highlight the very real differences in the social resources of these communities. Second, we examine the fiscal response to the QEA among these districts, and we answer the first research questions regarding the degree to which the QEA equalized revenues among these districts. Third, we describe the political and administrative contexts in which decisions were made that affected the four capacities for delivering education, and we explore how state policies, particularly state oversight procedures, changed these administrative contexts.

COMMUNITY CONTEXT

Although New Jersey is a major industrial state in the heart of the northeast corridor, it is, nonetheless, composed of quite distinct small towns and cities.

The salience of local communities in all aspects of civic life is substantial, perhaps in no area more so than in education, as attested to by the hundreds of local school districts, many with fewer than 2,000 students. School district boundaries usually parallel local municipal boundaries, and regional districts often serve similar types of communities. It is in these hundreds of local contexts that the implementation of the QEA unfolds.

The community contexts of local school districts can be described and understood from various perspectives. Here we consider four major aspects of the community contexts: the size and rate of growth of the student population, the social and demographic background of students, the wealth available in the community, and patterns of community support for schooling. Each of these allows us to understand more fully the very real differences among the districts in our sample and the districts in the state. Moreover, each of these carries implications for the operation of local districts in the wake of the changes brought about by the QEA.

The size of the student population served by a district and its rate of growth are important factors to be considered in any examination of the local conditions for the delivery of educational services. Size can pose challenges to the coordination and delivery of the educational program. In New Jersey there is some correspondence between district size and the three categories of districts identified by the court decision and the QEA. Most of the special needs districts are among the largest in the state, although a few are fairly small. The large number of foundation aid districts range in size. Generally, the transition aid districts, the wealthiest districts in the state, tend to be small, with 5,000 or fewer students.

These general patterns among districts statewide are reflected somewhat in our case study sample districts. The six special needs districts in our case study sample ranged from 4,000 to 29,000 students. The two foundation aid districts had enrollments of 8,000 (TR1) and 11,000 (TR2), respectively and are among the larger foundation aid districts. As is the case statewide, the transition aid districts in our case study sample were generally smaller, varying from 2,000 to 5,000 students. Thus the larger special needs districts may confront more challenging coordination and management tasks than the generally smaller transition aid districts.

In addition to the size of a student population, the stability of that population can also pose a considerable challenge to district leaders. Enrollment changes have particularly strong effects on district efficiency; districts do not respond well to either expansion or contraction of enrollment (Cibulka, 1987; Lankford & Wyckoff, 1995). Enrollment drops leave districts with excess capacity in the form of buildings that are difficult to sell and staff to whom the district may have long-term obligations. Beyond a certain point, growth requires both staff expansion and the addition of facilities.

Five of our case study districts were essentially stable, with growth rates of 3% or less between 1990/91—the year before QEA was implemented—through 1993/94, but the other seven experienced growth from 10% to 17%. The growing districts were distributed across all three types of districts: three in the special needs districts, one foundation aid district, and three in the transition aid districts. This suggests that both rich and poor districts would need revenue increases to cope with growth before they could commit new funds to programmatic improvement.

In addition to variation in size and growth rates, our 12 case study districts differed dramatically in their social and demographic characteristics. Figure 3.1 shows the proportions of students in our 12 case study districts with characteristics that place them at greater than normal risk for school failure. In Chapter 6 we discuss the implications of these indicators for special school district efforts to address student needs. Here we present these data to demonstrate the tangible differences among the student populations in our 12 districts.

Overall, the special needs districts serve substantially more students with one or more at-risk characteristics. None of the special needs districts has fewer than 70% minority students; none of the non–special needs districts has more than 18% minority students. In the special needs districts no fewer than 34% of the students are from single-parent homes; in the non–special needs districts no more than 15% of the students are from single-parent homes. In the special needs districts no fewer than one-third of the adults have failed to complete their high school education; among non–special needs districts no more than 20% of the adults have failed to complete high school. The percentage of students with limited English proficiency in the special needs districts ranges from 3% in SN4 to 24% in SN2. Nearly one-half or more of the students in the special needs districts are eligible for free or reduced lunch, while no more than 8% of the students among the non–special needs districts are eligible. Thus, with the single exception of limited English proficiency where there is some overlap between special needs and non–special needs districts, the special needs districts serve substantially more students with these risk factors than the non–special needs districts. Such risk factors represent special needs for both the individual students and for the districts in which they are concentrated.

These distributions of characteristics signifying added risk of school failure are striking at the district level as Figure 3.1 clearly shows. However, the implications of these differences among the student populations in the different categories of districts are even more notable when we consider how they might be manifest at the classroom level. Figure 3.2 portrays the number of children in one special needs district (SN3) and one transition aid district (TR4), with each of 10 family, community, and student characteristics identified as leading to greater risk of educational failure.

FIGURE 3.1. *At-risk indicators for communities and students of the case study districts*

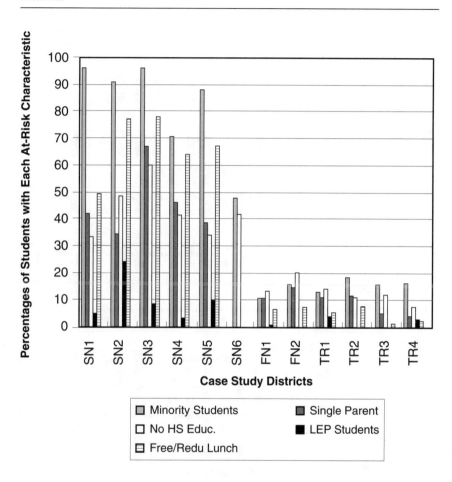

These differences are striking. Teachers in the poor district worked with much larger numbers of children who lived in poverty, had unemployed parents, lived in single-parent homes, and had parents who had not graduated from high school. The children in the poor district were somewhat more likely to have parents who did not speak English and to have limited English proficiency themselves. Moreover, teachers in the wealthy district could count on virtually all of their children to graduate high school while less than half in the poor district would do so.

FIGURE 3.2. *Number of children with disadvantaging characteristics in typical classes of 25 students in one special needs district and one transition aid district*

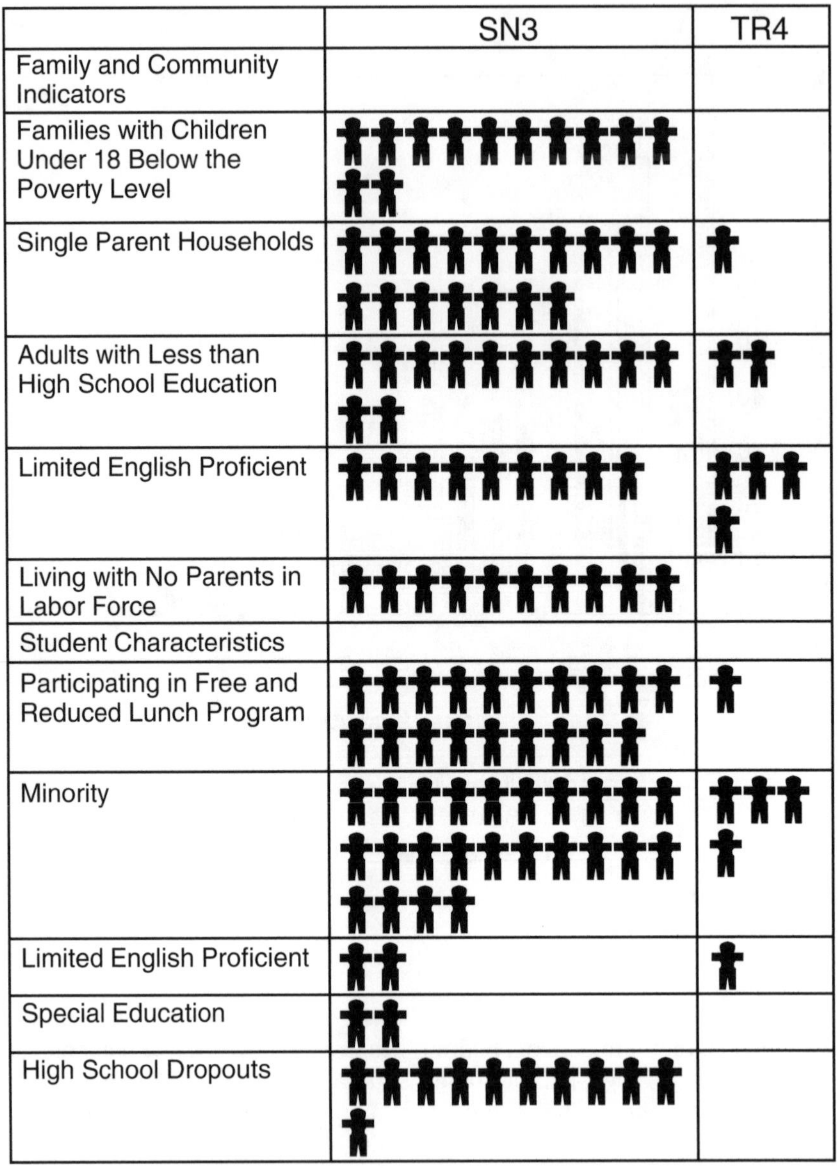

	SN3	TR4
Family and Community Indicators		
Families with Children Under 18 Below the Poverty Level	🧍🧍🧍🧍🧍🧍🧍🧍🧍🧍🧍 🧍🧍	
Single Parent Households	🧍🧍🧍🧍🧍🧍🧍🧍🧍🧍🧍🧍 🧍🧍🧍🧍🧍🧍🧍	🧍
Adults with Less than High School Education	🧍🧍🧍🧍🧍🧍🧍🧍🧍🧍🧍🧍 🧍🧍	🧍🧍
Limited English Proficient	🧍🧍🧍🧍🧍🧍🧍🧍🧍🧍🧍	🧍🧍🧍 🧍
Living with No Parents in Labor Force	🧍🧍🧍🧍🧍🧍🧍🧍🧍🧍🧍	
Student Characteristics		
Participating in Free and Reduced Lunch Program	🧍🧍🧍🧍🧍🧍🧍🧍🧍🧍🧍🧍 🧍🧍🧍🧍🧍🧍🧍🧍🧍🧍🧍	🧍
Minority	🧍🧍🧍🧍🧍🧍🧍🧍🧍🧍🧍🧍 🧍🧍🧍🧍🧍🧍🧍🧍🧍🧍🧍🧍 🧍🧍🧍🧍	🧍🧍🧍 🧍
Limited English Proficient	🧍🧍	🧍
Special Education	🧍🧍	
High School Dropouts	🧍🧍🧍🧍🧍🧍🧍🧍🧍🧍🧍 🧍	

These demographic differences were reflected in the day-to-day realities in these schools. Some educators with an historical perspective believed that these realities were getting worse. According to one elementary school principal from an urban district,

> We have children from dysfunctional families who have so many problems. There are lots of fights here; children have no respect for teachers. Discipline is a big issue. The children don't mean to be cruel, but they lack values and guidance. We need more one-on-one counseling for children. Counselors need time to deal with so many problems. This year alone four children were expelled.

Even when violence was not an issue, staff saw their students as facing numerous problems. The concept that *all* students in the special needs districts were at risk for one reason or another surfaced frequently in interviews. In contrast, field notes from one wealthy district described the district as follows:

> Employees of Bell Labs ... Prudential Insurance and other small technical-industrial companies live in this elegant suburban/rural town along with CEOs from Manhattan.... The children of these scientists and executives live in luxurious homes and are pressured by their successful parents to work hard in school. Ninety-six percent of the students go to college.

In another wealthy district, administrators explained that they designed their programs with the understanding that they were competing with the top private schools in the state. Available data on communities, data on the students attending the schools, and interviews with school staff, all reinforce the picture of dramatic differences among the students bodies served by the different kinds of school districts in our case studies.

These differences in the characteristics of students served by the different case study districts are mirrored by the wealth available to support schooling in those communities. The key measure of available wealth is equalized property valuation per pupil since local funding for education comes from property taxes. Among the six special needs districts, this figure ranged from $47,000 to $290,000. This means that support for the schooling of every pupil in these districts was derived from between $47,000 and $290,000 worth of property. The range among the four transition aid districts was from $627,000 to $1,136,000. Thus, the poorest of the rich districts had more than twice as much property wealth as the richest of the poor districts. The foundation aid districts we selected were closer to the state's poor districts than the wealthy ones in terms of of property wealth: their equalized valuation per pupil varied from $192,000 to $356,000, thus reminding us that a number of districts not counted among the state's poorest by the court faced significant fiscal constraints. The differences between the special needs districts and the transition aid districts in our case studies reflect patterns throughout the state; the average equalized valuation per pupil was $176,000 for the 30 special needs districts and $758,000 for the 108 wealthy districts, a fourfold difference.

A less material but no less important resource in local school districts is the level of community support for schools. Our case study districts experienced quite different patterns of community support. Most special needs districts had long histories of opposition to increasing school budgets, reflecting the already high tax rates occasioned by limited tax bases. This opposition may have been heightened by changing demographics in the communities. In most of the urban communities the minority population represented a much larger proportion of the school-age population than of the adult, tax-paying population. Thus, there seems to have been some sense that increasing support for schools would not be for "our kids." In at least two special needs districts, mayors actively campaigned against bond issues or increasing district operating budgets.

The notable exception to this pattern was one special needs district in which there was a close relationship between the city government and the school district administration. Here, however, the effects of a strongly cooperative relationship with the city leaders and general community support were mitigated by the very limited tax base that could be tapped to fund schools.

In contrast to the declining support for the schools in the special needs districts, the transition aid districts had long histories of community support for educational funding. Consensus on the importance of supporting schools was breaking down by the spring of 1991, however. In that year, the three transition aid districts (TR1, TR3, TR4) that required voter approval of budgets suffered defeats at the polls, two for the first time in many years. In the fourth district (TR2), school board members noted growing opposition to higher district budgets.

District administrators cited a number of reasons for the increased opposition to higher local funding: a growing percentage of senior citizens in some districts, a tightening economy that constrained family budgets, and resentment that teachers' salaries were rising at twice the rate of inflation, while many families found their own incomes stagnant. In addition, in the spring of 1991, Governor Florio and the president of the state senate publicly raised questions about the amount of waste in local school budgets a few weeks before local budget elections, thus bringing attention to these little-noticed events.

On the other hand, if support for educational expenditures was declining in the wealthy suburbs, it was still higher than in many poor urban districts. Some wealthy districts created education foundations that raised private funds to purchase computers and other equipment. Cases were successfully made for bond issues for new buildings in ways that had been nearly impossible in special needs districts for years. Thus, the wealthy districts faced new demands from their voters to demonstrate competent fiscal management, but they still had substantial reservoirs of public support.

The two middle-income districts showed a more mixed picture. In FN2, lack of community support rivaled what was found in the special needs districts. Annual budgets and bond issues to expand facilities had been voted down for years. As a result, district administrators resorted to legal expedients to cover building improvement costs, placing increased strains on the operating budget. During the study period, elected school board members became increasingly conservative fiscally, and the town government was unsupportive when it reviewed the local budget after voter defeats. According to district administrators, this general fiscal conservatism was part of a blue collar ethos that favored sports programs, secretaries, and maintenance staff (who lived in the community) over those same district administrators, who were viewed as overpaid outsiders. By contrast, FN1 was more like the wealthy districts. During the 1980s, voters passed both district budgets and bond issues to support expansion in this rapidly growing area, but in the early '90s community support declined and budgets began to fail, although not to the extent experienced in FN2.

In sum, although the growing numbers of students affected all three kinds of districts, the special needs districts served student populations with dramatically higher rates of characteristics associated with greater risk of school failure. These same districts had remarkably less property wealth than the transition aid districts, and endured substantially lower levels of community support. However, with growth creating challenges for districts at all levels, community patience with increasing costs was reaching its limits even in wealthier districts.

FISCAL CONTEXT

As a result of the passage of the QEA, all of the twelve local districts had additional funds to respond to both continuing and new demands. However, these new funds did not automatically flow to direct educational services for students; other calls were made upon these dollars. In this section we consider two major kinds of claims made upon the new resources: local tax relief and other needs for resources within local districts.

Expenditures versus Tax Relief

School districts draw on three sources of revenues to support their educational programs and services: federal, state, and local aid. Federal aid plays a minor role in education funding in New Jersey, providing, on average, only 4% of the state's education revenues. As discussed in Chapter 2, under the QEA the allocation of state aid was driven by the relative wealth and level of student need in a school district. The interaction of community wealth and tax effort determined the local education revenue available to a school district. Spending caps also affected how much a school district could increase its budget in any given year.

The impact of increased state education aid on school district spending is thus influenced by three factors: the size of the state aid increase, local taxing decisions, and the limits imposed by expenditure caps. Studies from the 1970s found that school districts increased educational expenditures between 50 and 85 cents for every additional dollar of general state aid (Odden & Picus, 1992). These studies did not, however, look at the impact of large increases in state aid that resulted from reformed school-funding formulas. When Goertz (1979) examined district response to New Jersey's 1975 school finance reform, she found that districts that received substantial increases in state aid (exceeding 25% of their budgets) spent, on average, 84% of their new funds on education. The remaining dollars were used to reduce property tax rates by an average of 20%. Low-spending and low-wealth districts directed relatively more of their new funds to education than did those that were more affluent and higher spending.

Table 3.1 shows the changes in education revenues in the sample districts under the 3 years of the QEA. State aid increased between 42% and 116% in the six poor urban districts (SN1 to SN6). All districts except SN5 allocated nearly all of their new aid to education expenditures, enabling them to increase education spending between 29% and 63% in that 3-year period (the equivalent of an annual growth rate of 9% to 18%). Four of these five districts used remaining dollars for a small property tax reduction (SN1, SN2, SN3, SN4). SN5 allocated more funds to property tax relief than the other districts. SN6 raised its property taxes substantially.

A major factor that affected the response of the poor urban districts was the "fair share" contribution requirement of the QEA. Each district was required to contribute in local tax dollars an amount that reflected its relative property and income wealth. The local fair share for special needs districts was set in 1992/93 at the lower amount of a district's 1990/91 tax levy or 117.65% of the state average school tax rate. If the state expenditure cap prevented the district from spending up to the foundation amount, its required fair share was reduced proportionately. This mandate put a floor on how much tax relief the special needs districts could take under the QEA.

The two foundation aid districts received increases in state aid of 37% and 30%, respectively. Over this 3-year period local revenues increased by 29% and 16%, respectively. These combined revenues produced overall rev-

TABLE 3.1. *Changes in education revenues, by category, 1990/91 to 1993/94*

| DISTRICT | STATE AID | | LOCAL REVENUES | | TOTAL REVENUES[a] | |
	PER PUPIL	% CHANGE	PER PUPIL	% CHANGE	PER PUPIL	% CHANGE
SN1	$2,001	42%	–$25	–1%	$1,977	29%
SN2	3,314	116	–177	–6	3,138	53
SN3	3,693	77	–111	–12	3,582	63
SN4	2,767	71	–107	–7	2,660	50
SN5	2,346	68	–669	–20	1,677	25
SN6	2,655	48	562	27	3,217	42
FN1	1,283	37	756	29	2,039	34
FN2	747	30	752	16	1,499	21
TR1	43	4	672	8	715	7
TR2	15	2	1,577	19	1,592	18
TR3	–55	–6	1,463	22	1,408	19
TR4	–30	–4	856	11	825	9

[a] Total general fund revenues.
Source: School District Advertised Budgets, Spring 1992 and Spring 1994. 1990/91 figures based on actual expenditures; 1993/94 based on revised appropriations.

enue increases of over 34% and 21% in the two districts. This meant that the districts could increase their spending each year an average of 10% and 7%, respectively.

The four wealthy districts had small changes in state aid, ranging from a loss of 6% of aid to an increase of 4%. Since state aid represents less than 10% of these districts' budgets, the dollar changes were also small, ranging from an increase of $43 per pupil to a loss of $55 per pupil. Not surprisingly, these districts raised their local taxes so they could maintain growth in their school budgets of between 2% and 6% a year.

When the QEA was enacted, suburban districts worried that the more restrictive budget caps included in the legislation would force them to "level down" the quality of their educational programs. We found, however, that only one of the four wealthy districts in our sample spent the amount allowed in its cap. Tight economic times coupled with taxpayer discontent and budget defeats at the polls, more than the caps, led the other districts to develop much more austere budgets than in the past.

How Districts Distributed New Funds

How did these districts allocate their new dollars in the period 1990/91 to 1993/94? Table 3.2 shows the percentage of increased expenditures allocated to six major spending categories:

1. Direct educational expense—instruction, attendance and health services, student body activities, special education and other special needs programs
2. Plant operation and maintenance
3. Transportation
4. Fixed charges and other expenses—including administration, community services, sundry accounts, and insurance costs
5. Tuition for out-of-district placements
6. Capital outlay

We included capital outlay in these analyses for two reasons. One is technical. When the state changed its accounting system in 1993/94 to conform to Generally Accepted Accounting Principles (GAAP), it moved certain categories of capital outlay expenditures from the instructional to the capital outlay category. Thus we needed to look at both categories to measure real change between 1990/91 and 1993/94. Second, and more important, we found that several of our special needs districts used new aid dollars to address years of neglect in their facilities and to purchase much-needed technology. These expenditures will show up in the capital outlay accounts. Two districts (SN6 and TR 4) were excluded because we could not get complete budget data in line item format for both years.

Regardless of district type, about half the increased funds were used for direct educational expenditures. The poor urban districts, on average, put 51% of new funding into direct educational expenses. The foundation aid districts put 65% and 66% of new funds into direct educational expenses. The wealthy districts, on average, put 62% of new funds into educational expenditures, but there was a real difference between two districts (TR1, TF3) that allocated 54% and 56% of new funds to this category—a figure comparable to most of our poor urban districts—and one (TF2) that spent 83% of its new dollars this way. All types of districts also had to use substantial portions of their new dollars for fixed costs: 17% in the poor urban districts; 10% in the foundation aid districts; and 35% in the wealthy districts.

There were differences in the proportions of new dollars added to operations and maintenance, fixed charges, and capital outlay. The poor urban districts spent an average of 9% of their new dollars on operation and maintenance, 17% on fixed charges, and another 11% on capital outlay. The two foundation aid districts kept operations and maintenance relatively stable, spend-

TABLE 3.2. *Changes in education expenditures, by category, 1990/91 to 1993/94*

DISTRICT	CHANGES IN CURRENT AND CAPITAL EXPENSE PER PUPIL	PERCENT OF EXPENDITURES ALLOCATED TO EACH CATEGORY					
		DIRECT EDUCATION EXPENSE[a]	OPERATION MAINTENANCE	TRANSPORTATION	FIXED CHARGE/ OTHER[b]	TUITION	CAPITAL OUTLAY
SN1	$2,323	46	10	2	15	16	9
SN2	3,056	44	3	3	31	8	10
SN3	3,692	57	10	3	14	3	12
SN4	2,883	53	5	1	22	4	14
SN5	1,921	53	11	2	15	8	11
SN6[c]							
FN1	2,413	65	2	1	15	2	15
FN2[d]	1,243	66	1	4	5	15	13
TR1	951	56	−30	−3	44	12	20
TR2	1,443	83	−9	1	18	4	4
TR3	1,531	54	1	1	31	7	5
TR4[e]	810						

Source: School district advertised budgets, Spring 1992 and Spring 1994. 1990/91 figures based on actual expenditures; 1993/94 figures based on revised appropriations.

[a] Direct education expenses are defined as the sum of the following budget line items: instruction, attendance and health services, student body activities, special education and other special needs programs.

[b] Fixed charges and other are the sum of budget lines for administration, community services, sundry accounts, and insurance costs. It excludes teacher retirement and Social Security costs.

[c] Incomplete data available for this district.

[d] Percentages add to more than 100% due to adjustment in payments to special schools.

[e] Comparable figures were not available for this district because it uses program, rather than line item, budgeting.

ing just 2% and 1% of their new dollars on this category. These districts devoted 15% and 5% of the additional expenditures to fixed charges and 15% and 13% to capital outlay. In contrast, two wealthy districts (TR1, TR2) reduced operations and maintenance costs by 30% and 9%, and a third wealthy district increased operations and maintenance by only 1%. These three transition aid districts devoted 44%, 18%, and 31% of additional expenditures, respectively, to fixed charges and 20%, 4%, and 5% of additional expenditures to capital outlay.

In dollar terms, spending on the direct education expense category increased an average of $1,350 in the poor urban districts, almost twice as much as that in the wealthy districts ($743). The foundation aid districts spent an additional $1,568 and $820 on direct education expense.

It is not surprising to find the poor urban districts increasing their investment in facilities and equipment in the early years of the QEA. Years of tight budgets had resulted in extensive deferred maintenance, hard use of school buildings, and pent-up demands for instructional equipment. SN2, for example, had already developed a wide variety of education and social support programs in the years preceding the QEA. While its students were successful on state tests, the community opposed extensive investment in education. Buildings were in sorry shape. And the district had no room to house growing enrollments and expanded programs. This district made a major investment in improving its facilities. SN4 had also had a difficult time convincing its overburdened and increasingly elderly taxpayers to fund improvements to its schools. QEA dollars, along with other state funds, were used to bring schools up to the standards of the building code, modernize science laboratories, and build libraries for its elementary schools.

In summary, the six special needs districts in the study received large increases in state aid and used most of these new funds to increase education expenditures, not to reduce taxes. Like their wealthier neighbors, the poor urban districts spent about half of their new revenues on instruction, programs for special needs students, and student support services. The urban districts also invested new state aid in facilities and equipment, addressing years of deferred spending in these areas. Some of the wealthy districts, constrained by small increases in state aid and taxpayer discontent, reduced spending on operations and maintenance to protect their instructional budgets.

ADMINISTRATIVE CONTEXT

In the preceding two sections we established the demographic and fiscal differences among the twelve case study districts, particularly as those differences distinguished the three types of districts. In this section we examine the differences among districts in their administrative arrangements, including the stability and shared perspective of administrative personnel and the level of autonomy of personnel at the school building level. We also consider the evolving state role in the oversight of local districts, especially the development of a differentiated strategy for monitoring the work of different types of districts.

While earlier research on implementation emphasized how local decision makers undermine the intent of central policy (Berman & McLaughlin, 1976), more recent research suggests that local efforts can also enhance the intended effects of such policies (Fuhrman, Clune, & Elmore, 1988). Relatively little is known about what separates districts that make constructive use of policies from those that do not. However, in reviewing a number of studies of district contributions to change, Fullan (1991) suggests that local school districts that support sustained improvement have cultures where values are shared and emphasize both student learning and caring for stake holders; there is frequent, fairly honest two-way communication; and bureaucratic constraints are minimized. This view agrees with earlier work of Berman and McLaughlin (1979), who suggest, among other things, that districts that support improvement allow for internal diversity, promote effective upward and downward communication in a climate of mutual trust, and emphasize service delivery over political and bureaucratic concerns. While such districts are neither strictly centralized nor decentralized, they do allow a good deal of school and teacher autonomy in a context where basic purposes are broadly shared. In addition to these general characteristics, it seems likely that such cultures are more likely to support rather than oppose policy when the district's goals are perceived to fit with the intent of the policy (Firestone, 1989). It should be noted that this image of effective district organization is rather different from the kind of central controls often promoted by those interested in efficiency and accountability.

Stability

One factor likely to affect the development of such a shared perspective or culture among staff in a local school district is the extent of administrative turnover. Fullan (1991) suggests that the average tenure of an American superintendent is three years. While turnover can stimulate by bringing in new blood, too frequent or poorly managed turnover can undermine the trust and easy communication that characterize districts that support change.

Table 3.3 provides a brief overview of the administrative context of each district. With regard to turnover, what is particularly striking is that only three districts had the same superintendent for all three years of the study, and two of those had a change just before the study began. Such turnover is consistent with Fullan's (1991) findings. However, in many of these districts that did experience turnover in the superintendency, there was stability. In

TABLE 3.3. *The administrative context of the 12 case study districts*

District	Administrative Turnover	Administrative Culture
SN1	3 external superintendents in 3 years	Turf warfare between offices—especially finance and program—and among individuals. No shared vision. Disorganized relations with schools.
SN2	Central administration together for years. New superintendent brings new blood.	Consensus on building strong academic programs. Unwillingness to address facilities problem until new superintendent arrives. Fairly decentralized.
SN3	Central administration together for years. New superintendent promoted from within.	General consensus that direction for change should include academic improvement and social programs.
SN4	Central administration together for years, but near retirement. Top leaders replaced in third year.	Fairly centralized. General consensus on direction for change. History of early childhood services. New $$ allows curricular improvement. Fairly centralized.
SN5	Clean sweep of central office before study started. Strong new team shakes up district, but its longevity questioned.	General consensus on direction for change in new team. Questions among old timers. Fairly centralized.
SN6	Long fight to remove superintendent. Then three superintendents in 3 years and central office reorganization.	Fragmented central office with most old timers waiting and protecting turf. Disagreement and turf wars.
FN1	Superintendent when QEA passed created some stability and added to central office staff, then left.	Reasonable consensus that major issue is dealing with growth. No internal fighting.
FN2	New superintendent at start of period but rest of central office stable.	Consensus on diverse mission maintained through ongoing strategic planning.

TR1	Long history of superintendent turnover. 1991 superintendent fired after falsifying building plan. Replacement hired from within to bring stability.	Consensus on approach to instruction. Positive relationships between district office and schools. Fairly decentralized.
TR2	Longtime superintendent replaced after a 1-year interim superintendent. No dramatic impact.	Decentralized approach to management but consensus on approach to instruction.
TR3	Previous superintendent replaced after a 1-year interim superintendent. Period of drift.	Drift and limited direction during turnover but no turf wars.
TR4	Same top leaders throughout.	Clear shared sense of purpose and sense of participating in cutting edge district.

SN2, SN4, and TR2 the change in the superintendent's office occurred after years of stability and was a generational changing of the guard. SN3, which had a well-integrated central administration that worked closely with its board, promoted from within in order to maintain stability.

The turnover experienced by these districts had both positive and negative effects. In SN2, the new superintendent brought a will to take on local opposition to badly needed building programs that had not been present before. On the other hand, the loss of a dynamic superintendent in SN1 followed by an interim superintendent and then a permanent one contributed to internal disarray. A long fight to remove a superintendent in SN6 followed again by an interim superintendent before a permanent one was hired had a similar effect. Superintendent turnover in TR3 also contributed to a period of drift and confusion, especially when the school board became more active in internal decision making. As is clear from Table 3.3, administrative stability was not related to district type among these twelve case study districts.

Shared Perspective

In examining administrative cultures in the case study districts through interviews with staff at all levels over three years, only three districts stand out as *not* having at least a reasonable level of consensus on purposes and capacity for internal communication. SN1 had a long history of conflicts between different departments in the central office and poor communication with the schools. Poor communication and protection of individual fiefdoms were also extensive in SN6. TR3 experienced a similar situation, although for a shorter period of time during a change of superintendents, in part because of how the superintendent at the beginning of the study left the district.

Autonomy

In light of Fullan's (1991) observations that the prevalence of school and teacher autonomy is conducive to continued improvement and constructive program implementation, the differences by district type in teachers' influence over district activities are notable. Table 3.4 shows teachers' reports of the amount of influence they have on curriculum, in-service priorities, and resource distribution in the twelve study districts.

In all three cases there is a significant difference in the reported influence of teachers in the special needs, foundation aid, and transition aid districts. Teachers in the special needs districts consistently have the least influence, while those in the transition aid districts have the greatest influence. These differences are paralleled in the statewide survey of superintendents by differences in their reports of teacher influence over policy in rich and poor districts.

TABLE 3.4. *Teacher-reported influence on aspects of school operations by district type*

SCHOOL OPERATION	SPECIAL NEEDS		FOUNDATION		TRANSITION	
	MEAN	N	MEAN	N	MEAN	N
Curriculum	2.46***	1,239	2.94***	221	3.27***	399
In-service priorities	1.96***	1,234	2.21***	221	2.78***	395
Resource distribution within the school	2.02***	1,231	2.18***	222	2.57***	398

Responses: 1 = none, 2 = a little, 3 = moderate amount, 4 = a great deal.
$*p < .05$ $**p < .01$ $***p < .001$

State Oversight

QEA brought with it new procedures and policies for oversight of the special needs districts that along with the vestiges of the earlier monitoring processes ensured that the urban districts would get more direction (and also somewhat more support) from the department of education than the other districts (see Chapter 2). Governor Florio argued that such oversight would promote efficiency and accountability. In this section we explore the extent to which this oversight contributed to such efficiency and also excellence. Our conclusions are decidedly mixed. State oversight did have benefits by surfacing problems that communities had tried to ignore, motivating the most internally divided districts to action, and providing assistance in adopting specific programs. However, it could not help districts develop the high trust, high consensus, high communication culture that Fullan (1991) suggests contributes to effective improvement. Moreover, there were costs in the form of time redirected from improvement to coping with the state and lost school and teacher autonomy.

EFFECTS ON LOCAL ADMINISTRATION

In some special needs districts the QEA oversight did contribute to efficiency. In SN1, for instance, where rapid executive succession combined with extensive internal conflict and poor internal communication, the outgoing superintendent had pushed for a challenging first-year plan for use of QEA funds. After she left, no one was committed to the plan. Partly as a result of internal conflicts, funds were not released to support the start-up of planned new activities. State monitors identified the problem, initiated an audit, and took other steps to ensure that some action was taken. They also ensured that a less-ambitious, more realistic plan would be developed for the second year. Without oversight, it is quite likely that nothing would have been done with QEA funds in the first year. Yet, because this oversight could not solve the fundamental problem of a divisive internal culture, extensive state intervention continued to be necessary to achieve fairly modest change.

QEA oversight also contributed to improvement in districts with more cohesive cultures by publicizing problems and providing additional assistance. For instance, the state external review team was instrumental in documenting and publicizing serious facilities problems in SN2. Its work focused the new superintendent's attention on that area and provided help in getting community support for the bond issue that eventually funded major building renewal efforts. SN3 became the biggest user of the state's programmatic assistance, most notably to implement the school reform ideas of Comer (1996). It did so, however, in large part because that program fit well with the superintendent's goal of providing improved social services for the city's poverty-stricken children.

However, the state oversight itself contributed to a kind of waste and inefficiency. Meeting the state reporting requirements required considerable time and energy of administrators in the special needs districts. Each district wrote several objectives for its Education Improvement Plan (EIP; see Chapter 2). District staff then divided each objective into multiple activities and sub-activities, and specified a resource person for the activity, persons responsible for the activity, date, and cost. The resulting documents were quite large, with representative EIPs generally over 200 pages long.

In the first year, the unstable policy context of revisions to the QEA and reductions in funding for poor urban districts compounded the problems of generating EIPs. These changes prompted three reactions among district staff. The first was anger and disappointment as expectations were raised and then dashed. The second was a common perception that the new state oversight procedures were a waste of time. Informants in one district reported that in the first year they had to revise their plan five times. The third was an unwillingness to make major program commitments or hire staff for fear that the state might soon take away the money. Thus, instability surrounding funding constrained planning. The short-term instability of the first year was not repeated, but every year the state changed its oversight procedures, and adapting to these changes required additional time of district administrators. Beginning in the second year, the state required each school to develop its own plan as well, so teachers' time was also involved. Finally, monthly visits by department liaisons consumed even more time.

Not surprisingly, the special needs districts spent more time dealing with state oversight than any of the other districts. Special needs districts were visited by external review teams shortly after the QEA was enacted. They submitted annual plans and underwent monthly site visits to ensure that funds were not misspent (even though they were not the only districts getting increases in state funding). In contrast, middle-income and wealthy districts had little contact with the department. One administrator in a wealthy district found the concept of state monitoring "bizarre" in light of his assumption that his district was better able to assess and implement effective programs than state staff. In another district, our site visitor wrote, "No one remembers when the state monitors were here last, no one knows when they will return, and no one really cares."

Data from our statewide surveys of superintendents confirmed the reports of administrators in our case study districts. Superintendents in special needs districts reported that they spent eleven days per month "responding to mandates for reporting to state government authorities" as opposed to seven days in foundation aid districts and six in transition aid districts. They also reported that other central office staff spent fourteen days on such reports in special needs districts as opposed to ten days in foundation aid districts and nine in transition aid districts.

EFFECTS ON LOCAL AUTONOMY

The expectation on the part of the general public that the state would exercise greater oversight in special needs districts appears to be in tension with the research literature on school improvement, which suggests that greater local autonomy and reduced bureaucratic constraints are more likely to lead to sustained efforts for genuine improvement. Our finding that teachers in the special needs districts report the least autonomy and superintendents in those districts report the most contact with state officials caused us to examine more closely the possible relationship between state oversight and the creation of conditions for local school improvement.

It is difficult to attribute differences in reported teacher autonomy solely to state oversight because similar differences in teacher influence between urban and suburban districts have been identified in national samples and in other parts of the country (Hannaway, 1993; Witte & Walsh, 1990). Nevertheless, state oversight appears to be a contributing factor. Organizational theorists argue that in the presence of external threats, organizations will centralize control in order to protect core production processes, including instruction, from outside interference. Such centralization provides for a uniform response that is well calibrated to the nature of the threat.

Additional data from our statewide survey of superintendents indicate that superintendents from poor urban districts see the state as a potential threat. When asked how much their district is affected by changes in state funding—on a scale where 1 means "not at all affected" and 5 means "greatly affected"—superintendents from special needs districts reported the greatest effect (4.80) followed by those from foundation aid (4.37) and transition aid (4.03) districts. Table 3.5 shows how much influence superintendents think that state government in general and state monitoring in particular have over four kinds of decisions:

1. *Program content* including course content, courses offered, kinds of texts, and teaching materials
2. *Program scope*, including the kind and extent of educational and other services offered to students
3. *Total resources available*, or the complete pool of resources available to support the district's operation
4. *Resource allocations*, or the distribution of district resources among competing needs

In six of eight possible instances, superintendents in special needs districts perceive that the state has more influence on decisions than do those from foundation aid and transition aid districts. In fact, responses are typically ordered so that superintendents from special needs districts perceive the greatest state influence and those from transition aid districts perceive the least. In four of the eight instances, the differences are statistically significant at or below the .05 level and on a fifth item, the influence of state monitoring on

TABLE 3.5. *Influence of state on aspects of local operations by distict type*

	SPECIAL NEEDS		FOUNDATION		TRANSITION	
	MEAN	N	MEAN	N	MEAN	N
Influence of state government						
Program content	3.58	12	3.68	103	3.39	90
Program scope	3.92*	12	3.42*	104	3.17*	91
Total resources	4.17***	12	3.96***	104	3.07***	90
Resource allocations	3.50***	12	3.27***	104	2.58***	90
Influence of state monitoring						
Program content	3.91	11	3.73	103	3.46	91
Program scope	3.83	12	3.75	101	3.39	92
Total resources	2.92	12	2.91	103	2.57	91
Resource allocations	3.17*	12	2.98*	103	2.59*	90

Responses: 1 = not at all influential; 5 = extremely influential
* $p > .05$, ** $p > .01$, *** $p > .001$

program scope, the difference just misses statistical significance.

These data suggest that while the QEA, and earlier Chapter 212, helped to reduce fiscal inequities, the oversight procedures associated with these laws may have contributed to inequities in another area: district and teacher autonomy. If we accept the argument of those who have studied school reform that such autonomy is a key ingredient of efforts to mount sustained school improvement efforts, then the verdict on the increased oversight that accompanied the QEA must be open at this point in the process.

It is useful to review our findings regarding the administrative context in light of the public expectations about the management of rich and poor districts cited from the newspaper sources in Chapter 1. Public expectations were that the poor urban districts were badly managed while the opposite was likely to be true of wealthy districts. For the most part, our exploration does not support such expectations. In four of the six special needs districts, there was a reasonable level of trust as well as clear consensus on how to move forward. SN2 had a long history of developing and effectively implementing quality instructional programs for its students although it had not addressed a serious facilities problem. The superintendent of SN3 promoted a vision for improvement that focused on both improved instruction and extensive development of social programs so that schools would become "oases in the ghetto." SN4 had pioneered the use of early childhood education and had a clear knowledge of the programs that had been cut as a result of past budget problems and needed to be reinstated. The new administrative team in SN5 also promoted a vision of academic improvement and early childhood education. If the rest of the administration held back to see how well the new team would do, there appeared to be little opposition or sabotage. In all four districts, the backlog of unmet needs (Kirst, 1977) provided a direction for the new funding that became available. The exceptions were SN1 and SN6, which better fit the stereotypical image of the divided, bureaucratic, urban school district. In spite of these two districts, the prevalence of special needs districts that had at least reasonable consensus on direction and internal communication is worth noting.

The non–special needs districts in our sample, while not displaying problems as pronounced as those in SN1 and SN6, were not without their own management problems. The leadership in FN2 had not been able to mobilize community support to address growing deficiencies in district resources and programs. TR3, because of the period of administrative drift during the years of our study, no doubt missed opportunities to make improvements. Overall, the distribution of management talent and dedication appears not to be related to the type of district, at least in our limited sample.

CONCLUSIONS

In this chapter we have examined the very real differences in the communities and student populations served by the twelve case study districts. This examination shows that the poor urban districts face greater educational challenges with fewer financial resources than their wealthy suburban counterparts. Analysis of fiscal changes shows that the poor urban districts invested most of the new money made available to them in categories directly related to education. One notable exception was funds used for property tax relief. This use was mandated by budget caps and reflected the greater effort to support education made by taxpayers in those districts. Another was the larger investment in maintenance and capital expenditures in light of years of infrastructure decay in those districts.

We have also shown how differences in the administrative contexts and the differential application of state oversight combined both to foster and to constrain school improvement. Our review suggests that the generally accepted belief that urban districts are more poorly administered than suburban ones is probably overstated and may result in part from state actions intended to improve the administration in just those districts. In the chapters to come we show how school districts in these disparate local settings reacted to the state actions flowing from the QEA to address the needs of their students.

4

PERSONNEL CHANGES

W ith this chapter we begin the analysis of the second research question: how much did changed expenditure patterns equalize districts' capacities to provide a quality education to students? We focus on personnel because the largest portion of school district budgets goes to salaries. In 1990/91, 57% of current education expenditures (and 84% of instructional expenditures) was allocated to staff salaries (Raimondo, 1994). Therefore, much of how resource allocation decisions affect instruction is through the purchase of personnel.

Analyses of personnel patterns especially help illuminate issues related to equity and efficiency. We address equity issues by comparing staffing patterns in rich and poor districts. Comparisons of both staff characteristics and the ratios of the numbers of staff to the numbers of students are presented. We address efficiency issues by examining how staff are distributed across categories. This allows us to consider the extent to which districts employ administrators and other nonteaching categories of personnel, personnel often deemed by the public to be tangential to the educational process. In the process of addressing these issues, we clarify how a number of factors—including demographic changes, salary agreements, and district culture—affect personnel decisions.

Because the salary system for educators tends to reward longevity and course taking (Firestone, 1994), we assumed that new funding would do most to improve instruction through hiring new personnel. Therefore, we first analyzed how new funds were distributed between salary increases for existing staff and hiring new staff. Next, because of the controversies over salary increases, we compared raises in wealthy, suburban, and poor urban districts to see whether higher salaries helped purchase stronger staff in terms of experience and formal education. Finally, we examined changes in staffing patterns to see how fiscal changes affected those patterns and how comparable patterns were across districts at the end of three years.

The major data source was information collected by the state on certified personnel—that is, teachers, administrators, and such educational services staff as counselors and librarians. The state files provide data on each person's position, salary, years of experience, and education. These data also allowed us to compare patterns in our 12 districts with the broader patterns for the 30 special needs districts and the 108 wealthiest districts in the state. For noncertified personnel, we used information collected by the New Jersey Education Association. These archival data were supplemented with qualitative information gained through site visits.

SALARY INCREASES VERSUS ADDITIONAL STAFF

Additional personnel dollars may be spent either on increased salaries for existing staff or on increasing staff numbers. Dollars devoted to raises for existing staff may do little to improve the educational process, particularly if staff are asked to do nothing new. Dollars allocated to the hiring of new staff may at least improve the ratios of staff to students.

To determine the distribution of funds between salary increases for existing staff and the hiring of new personnel, we first computed the total increase in salaries from 1990 to 1993. Next, we computed the average salary increase and multiplied that by the number of people on staff in 1990 to get the total salary increases for existing staff. The amount spent on new personnel was the difference between the total salary increase and the amount spent on raises.

Table 4.1 shows that our six special needs districts increased personnel spending by $835 per 1993 pupil compared to an increase of $580 in the four transition aid districts. Thus the special needs districts increased personnel spending 44% more than the transition aid districts. Moreover, the poor districts spent less on salary increases and more on hiring new staff than did the wealthy districts. It appears that within the constraints of existing salary agreements, special needs districts made a major effort to hire new staff. In contrast, the amount spent on new personnel in the transition aid districts is negative, indicating that staff had to be let go.

While raising salaries so much that staff had to be let go seems irrational, wealthy districts had relatively little short-run discretion. All professional salaries in these districts were geared to teacher contracts agreed to for 3-year periods. As a result, patterns of raises followed decisions made before the Quality Education Act (QEA) went into effect. District TR3, for instance, reached a settlement with its teachers in 1990/91, the year before QEA, that gave teachers annual salary increases of 8.2%. When QEA was passed the

TABLE 4.1. *Distribution of new salary funds between salary increases and new staff in special needs and transition districts, (in dollars per 93 pupil), 1990/1993*

DISTRICTS	TOTAL CHANGE	SALARY INCREASES	NEW STAFF	
			AMOUNT	PERCENTAGE
Case Study				
Special needs	$835	$570	$268	32%
Transition aid	580	634	–90	–16
Statewide				
Special needs	756	637	119	16
Transition aid	775	697	78	10

next year, the state capped increases on its budget to 6% per year. Thus for 2 years, the district would have had to get special voter approval to raise its budget enough to cover its contract. When a new agreement was reached beginning in the 1993/94 school year, increases were set in the 4.2% to 4.8% range. Generally, as settlements were reached during this period, the size of increases went down in both rich and poor districts, but there were often discontinuities for a few years that forced districts—especially the wealthier ones that had lower budget caps and little support to override those caps—to reduce staff to balance the budget.

The districts in our case study sample accentuate statewide patterns because our poor urban districts were somewhat poorer and lower spending than the 30 special needs districts overall, while the wealthy districts were wealthier and higher spending than the 108 wealthy districts. Statewide, rich and poor districts increased their spending on salaries for certified staff about the same amount per pupil. However, the special needs districts put somewhat less money into salary increases and more into new hires. The poor districts put 16% of new salary dollars into new staff, while the wealthy districts spent 10% in the same way. Thus, while most wealthy districts did not have to reduce staff, they still spent less per pupil on new staff than did the poor districts during this 3-year period.

SALARY CHANGES

Increasing the number of educational personnel in a district can contribute to the educational process if new people help reduce class size (Mosteller, 1995; Odden, 1990), but certain dimensions of staff quality are also important. Salaries are important to a district because they contribute to its relative advantage in attracting and retaining quality staff. Table 4.2 shows the salary increases for three categories of personnel—teachers, administrators, and educational services personnel—during the study period. In the sample districts, salary increases were at best only marginally larger in poor districts than in rich ones. For instance, teachers' salaries increased 5.6% over the 3-year period in the six poor urban districts as opposed to 5.23% in the wealthy districts. This essential equity in salary increases coexists with a substantial base inequity in salaries that preceded the QEA and existed afterwards. Thus, before the QEA, teachers in the poor urban districts made 24% less than teachers in wealthy districts, and administrators in the poor districts made 27% less than their counterparts in wealthy districts. These differences were essentially the same three years later. Statewide, the underlying differences in salaries are somewhat smaller—13% between teachers in wealthy and poor urban districts, and 16% between administrators—but every bit as stable.

TABLE 4.2. *Mean salaries for teachers, administrators, and educational services personnel, 1990 and 1993, in special needs districts and transition aid districts (case study sample and statewide)*

| | | SALARY | | ANNUALIZED |
PERSONNEL	DISTRICTS	1990	1993	PERCENT CHANGE
Teachers				
Case study	Special needs	$35,643	$41,971	5.60%
	Transition aid	44,533	51,889	5.23
Statewide	Special needs	37,606	44,370	5.67
	Transition aid	42,616	50,296	5.68
Administrators				
Case study	Special needs	53,968	63,755	5.71
	Transition aid	69,142	80,791	5.33
Statewide	Special needs	57,925	68,033	5.51
	Transition aid	67,104	78,626	5.42
Educational Services Personnel				
Case study	Special needs	41,544	47,540	4.60
	Transition aid	49,475	56,094	4.27
Statewide	Special needs	41,783	48,843	5.34
	Transition aid	45,103	53,596	5.92

While salary differences may be attributable in part to differences in experience and education of teachers in wealthier districts, personal background factors do not fully explain the difference. Using regression analysis, we determined that the average salary difference between teachers in rich and poor urban districts throughout the state in 1993/1994 was $3,271, after controlling for variation in experience and education. The difference for administrators was even higher— $9,249—and relatively more of the difference in salaries is explained by district wealth and less by personal characteristics than is true for teachers. Thus, three years of the QEA did little to reduce the salary gap between rich and poor districts.

Differences in salaries seemed to affect the quality of the teaching force. The superintendent of our smallest urban district, which had one of the lowest average teaching salaries, complained that his district had been the training ground for the surrounding districts for years. Teachers would begin in his district and after 2 or 3 years move to a neighboring district that offered higher salaries.

This anecdotal evidence is borne out by an examination of staff backgrounds. Statewide teachers in wealthy districts have about a year-and-a-half more experience (16.8 years' in wealthy districts versus 15.1 years' in poor urban districts), and about 2% fewer have 5 years' or less experience (18.2% in wealthy districts versus 20.4% in poor districts). An even bigger difference is apparent in formal education where 20% more teachers in wealthy districts have master's degrees (51.9% versus 31.3%). Again, these differences are somewhat larger in our sample districts. In our four wealthy districts, 17% have 5 years' or less experience compared to 22% in the six poor urban districts; twice as many teachers have master's degrees in our wealthy districts as in our poor ones (53.8% versus 27.2%).

The difference in experience between administrators in wealthy and poor districts is essentially negligible (24.4 years' experience in the poor urban districts versus 24.0 in the wealthy ones statewide), but that in education is noticeable. This is especially true at the doctoral level where more than twice as many administrators in wealthy districts have this degree as in poor districts. The pattern holds statewide (19.8% in wealthy districts; 8.9% in poor urban ones) and in our sample districts (23.3% versus 8.9%). Although almost all administrators have master's degrees, the tendency to have one is somewhat higher in the rich districts (96.9% versus 93.4% in the poor urban districts statewide). This difference is somewhat larger in our sample districts (90.5% of administrators have master's degrees in poor districts, while 95.1% do in wealthy districts). Similarly, educational services personnel tend to have the same level of experience in rich and poor districts, but more of them in wealthy districts have master's degrees. Statewide 81.6% of these personnel have master's degrees in wealthy districts as opposed to 69.7% in poor urban districts. In our sample districts, the percentages are 87.0 and 72.2, respectively.

These data are somewhat difficult to interpret on two grounds. Murnane (1995) suggests that master's and other advanced degrees are not necessarily related to improved teaching performance. More important indicators come from direct measures of teachers' verbal and other cognitive achievements. Moreover, it is difficult to know how much the differences in degrees received reflect salary incentives or the historically greater willingness of wealthy districts to fund teachers' continuing education by paying tuition for college courses. In addition, Murnane (1995) suggests, high salaries only improve the quality of the teaching force if administrators use the incentives at their disposal to hire the best talent. Poor hiring decisions lead to wasted resources.

Nevertheless, a conservative interpretation of the evidence presented on salaries and teacher characteristics suggests two important, continuing inequities between New Jersey's rich and poor districts. First, by paying higher salaries, the wealthy districts have greater access to the most effective teachers, should they choose to use the resources at their disposal wisely. Second, by pursuing higher degrees, staff from wealthier districts have access to more current knowledge about changes in educational practice, again if they choose their programs wisely.

More speculatively, for all the concern about financial mismanagement in poor urban districts at the time the QEA was passed, it appears that there is more potential for waste in the wealthy districts, if only because they spend more on salaries. This is evident in the comments of one superintendent in a transition aid district who explained that having ready resources for personnel allowed the district to avoid dealing with issues of poorly performing or difficult staff by assigning additional staff to the same tasks to make sure that they were accomplished. Evidence of using slack resources to avoid dealing with problems was also clear in the comments of one principal in this same district. He noted that the ambitious music program in his elementary school, which often involved students in a "regular music class, an instrumental lesson, and a choral music class after school in a single day," interfered with the basic program. This situation was allowed to continue because district administrators chose to avoid a confrontation with a music teacher who pursued his own interests and developed an overly elaborate music program for elementary school students.

CHANGES IN PERSONNEL

The public anticipated that urban districts would waste new funds in two ways: by spending excessively on teachers' salaries, which we have seen was not the case, and by hiring administrators who would not be teaching children. The consensus seemed to be that hiring teachers would be useful but hiring administrators and other nonteaching personnel would not. The research suggesting that, under certain conditions, smaller class sizes contribute to student achievement lends credence to this view (Mosteller, 1995; Odden, 1990). On the other hand, schools and districts must clearly accomplish a variety of nonteaching functions, from budgeting to continuing professional development. Since some of these things might best be done by teachers (arguably continuing professional development) and some not, the optimal mix of teaching and nonteaching personnel is not clear. Still, following public perception and the available research, the assumption guiding our analysis of personnel distribution was that generally the allocation of personnel to regular classroom teaching roles was the most efficient use of both new and old money.

As we have noted, all types of districts devoted comparable amounts of new dollars to salary increases, but poor districts invested more heavily in new staff than rich districts. This section both describes changes in personnel from 1990 to 1993 and compares staffing patterns at the end of the 3-year period. After providing a broad overview, more specific analyses are presented for teachers, administrators, and noncertified staff.

Changes in Certified Staff and Student Enrollment

Our poor urban districts increased staff across the board, but the biggest expansion was in educational services personnel (14%), with the ranks of teachers and administrators growing by 7% and 8%, respectively. We have pointed out that the wealthy case study districts increased salaries during this time more than they increased funding on staff overall, so they had to reduce staff. Generally, they held the line on teachers (1% increase) while reducing educational services staff somewhat (5%) and substantially shrinking the number of administrators (25%).

Once more the pattern evident among our case study districts is somewhat more extreme than in the state as a whole. Statewide, poor districts increased their educational services personnel by 11% and teachers by 5% while actually reducing administrators by 2%. Meanwhile, the rich districts statewide had a slightly larger increase of teachers (3%) and smaller reduction of administrators (a still-noticeable 10%) while actually increasing educational services staff by 3%.

The picture suggested by the percentage changes is excessively positive for both rich and poor districts, however, because it does not take population growth into account. During the 3 years of the study, student enrollment increased 6% in the sample poor urban districts. Thus, the apparently large growth in educational support staff (almost 100 people across the 6 districts) was essentially absorbed by population growth, resulting in an increase of only 0.65 staff per 1,000 students. Similarly, an increase of 374 teachers only enhanced the number of teachers per 1,000 students by 0.39 and the ratio of administrators per 1000 students only went up 0.12. Thus, the 6 poor districts in our case studies essentially held the line on personnel.

In the 4 wealthy case study districts the student population increased 9%. Although the change in number of teachers in those districts was minuscule, the number of teachers per 1,000 students actually declined by 5.35. The decreases in administrators and educational services personnel were 2.94 and 1.08 per 1,000, respectively.

Statewide, the growth in the student population was not as pronounced as in the case study districts, but it was still a noticeable 3% in the 30 poor urban districts and 7% in the wealthy ones. The full set of poor districts was somewhat more successful in raising the ratio of teachers to students registering an increase of 0.84 per 1,000. These districts actually reduced administrators by 0.35 per 1000 students, and increased educational services staff by 0.65 per 1,000 students, the same amount as in our case study districts. In the transition aid districts statewide, the ratios of staff to students fell, but at smaller rates than in the 4 case study transition aid districts. Statewide, transition aid districts registered decreases in personnel per 1,000 students of 2.69 teachers, 1.33 administrators, and 0.27 educational services staff.

These averages hide important variations among districts within each category. In fact, as Table 4.3 shows, only three poor urban districts in the case study sample (SN3, SN4, SN6) showed measurable net increases in staff when enrollment changes are taken into account. Two (SN1, SN5) had a net loss of staff when small staff increases were overwhelmed by large enrollment growth. Their stories are similar to one transition aid district (TN2). In one special needs district (SN2) and one transition aid district (TN4), enrollment growth and staff increases essentially cancelled out. Finally, two transition aid districts (TN1, TN3) suffered a combination of staff reductions and enrollment growth. Thus, even some special needs districts experienced a net reduction in staff, and rich and poor districts alike that increased staff were not able to do so at a rate that kept pace with student growth.

The districts that increased staff responded to a variety of local priorities. For instance, SN3 added 137 teachers (11% increase), 17 administrators (10%), and 50 educational services staff (32% increase). One of the poorest districts in the country, its administration had a vision of making its schools into integrated social services centers to help overcome the economic depression and family dislocation so prevalent in surrounding neighborhoods. To that end, it initiated two elementary school programs, one working with the New Jersey Department of Education to introduce the Comer School Development Program and the other locally created. Both programs called for the expan-

TABLE 4.3. *Changes in student enrollment, teaching staff, and teachers per 1000 students in case study districts, 1990 to 1993*

DISTRICTS	PERCENT CHANGE IN STUDENT ENROLLMENT	PERCENT CHANGE IN TEACHING STAFF	CHANGE IN TEACHERS PER 1000 STUDENTS
SN1	12.13%	3.72%	–4.91
SN2	6.61	8.47	1.21
SN3	1.69	10.58	5.81
SN4	-0.68	13.41	9.71
SN5	10.01	2.92	–4.66
SN6	2.45	9.07	4.73
FN1	10.07	14.17	2.27
FN2	3.28	1.36	–1.34
TR1	9.96	–2.24	–8.60
TR2	13.20	7.65	–3.91
TR3	17.31	–0.60	–11.19
TR4	1.18	1.31	0.08

sion of social services staff—social workers, psychologists, and so forth—in schools. At the same time, SN3 initiated an integrated social services center at one of its high schools with district funds. This center was modeled on a similar pilot program in another high school that was supported with state funds. Along with these programs in regular schools, the district started an alternative school for especially difficult middle school–aged children.

SN3 increased services at the elementary level beyond the introduction of social services–oriented programs. Most new staff were placed at this level. In addition to those already mentioned, some were hired to expand the number of full-day kindergartens. Others were new librarians placed in schools that were getting libraries for the first time.

The district also increased staff to help regular classroom teachers. It placed at least one mentor teacher in each school. These were expert teachers without student assignments whose responsibility was to help beginning teachers and others who needed to improve their instruction. Principals also found these mentor teachers very helpful during a period where aggressive efforts were being made to improve the quality of instruction. One principal explained that the mentor teacher's job was to work primarily with beginning teachers, "but I will use him with all teachers. Nontenured and provisional teachers are his primary focus, but I may go into a tenured teacher's classroom and see that that teacher needs assistance. I will then turn to the mentor teacher." In addition, the district added assistant principals at the secondary level.

Although SN3 added a substantial number of staff in a variety of areas, these changes were made slowly. During the first year of the QEA, district administrators were reluctant to hire new people because they questioned whether funding increases from the state would remain stable. In fact, by the end of the study period, they reported that declining state aid might jeopardize efforts to keep all these new staff.

Several new hires in SN4 were replacements for staff who had been cut in early years of tight education budgets. This small district added 35 teachers and six support staff—all counselors—in the QEA period (13% and 17% increases, respectively). These changes reflected ongoing priories. One, as in SN3, was to increase support services for the large number of poor low-achieving students to increase attendance and reduce dropouts. Related to this, teachers in the high school who had been laid off earlier were replaced, and the district added a period to the high school schedule to allow students who needed remedial courses to pass the state's high school graduation test to take electives as well. Finally, teachers were added to respond to the growing number of limited English speakers and special education students.

Some poor districts initiated new programs even when staff increases did not keep up with enrollment growth. In SN5, for instance, a new administration had stepped into a district that had a history of bad management and significantly reduced the central office staff. Although most of this reduction took place before the QEA was passed, the district still managed to decrease its administrative staff by 20% during the QEA period. Simultaneously, it hired about three times as many teachers as the number of supervisors that were laid off. While most of these were used to address growing enrollments, the new superintendent gave top priority to expanding a small early childhood education program that had started shortly before the passage of the QEA. Preschool enrollment almost doubled from 219 to 412 between 1990 and 1993. Lacking space in its own schools, the district placed classrooms in available space in low-income housing projects. In the process, it added about 30 early childhood education teachers.

The wealthy districts that lost staff in relation to the number of students coped by reallocating resources. TN3, for instance, was overwhelmed by enrollment growth: a three-year, 17% expansion in the number of students with a 21% increase in grades K–3. While the district maintained the same number of staff positions, people were released to enable the district to hire more regular classroom teachers. Eliminating some of these positions increased the efficient use of funds. For instance, the district let go eight permanent substitutes who primarily coached sports teams and did not have regular teaching assignments. Other targeted staff had provided support to the regular educational program. In 1992/93, the district laid off three half-time teachers who worked in grades 4 and 5 as well as teachers of physical education, creative arts, and the academic enrichment program in the middle school. The district also sent a teacher who was serving as the audiovisual coordinator back to the classroom. These changes did impact on services somewhat. For instance, there was an initial dislocation in the use of audiovisual materials in the high school until a technician was hired. In addition, because staff could not keep up with growth in the number of special education students, the district tightened entry requirements into that program.

The reductions in staff-student ratios in TN1 were not as large as in TN3, but this district actually lost staff—including nine teachers, a 2% reduction. TN1 also reduced the number of administrators by seven (18%), and educational services staff by 6 (8%). This change actually includes a useful redirection of staff. In 1991/92, the district reduced its high school staff by 20 after consolidating two separate schools into one new building. It did so in part because high school enrollments were essentially stagnant. However, during the 3 years of the study, K–3 enrollments increased 16%, and the district was able to hire some new teachers to address this growth.

TN2 added dramatically to its staff overall, but it still could not keep up with its population growth. This small district added 14 teachers, but it did so in part by reducing educational services staff and central office administrators. Here too, some useful belt tightening resulted. In one elementary school we visited, the only staff change was the loss of the music teacher running the overly ambitious program described earlier. On visiting the school, we had expected the principal to complain at least a little about this loss. Instead, he was relieved.

In sum, changes in numbers of staff have to be interpreted in light of demographic shifts that cut across district wealth. The poor urban districts that had the net staff additions benefited not only from increased state aid under the QEA, but also from stable enrollments. Other poor and wealthy districts saw their revenue increases absorbed by student growth, and a few wealthy districts suffered from simultaneous staff losses (because funds had to be allocated to salary increases) and enrollment increases. The consequences of belt tightening in the wealthy districts varied from case to case. In some cases, new financial stringencies forced useful economies. In others, population growth appeared to overwhelm the district and undermine the quality of services.

Noncertified Staff

Although the state does not collect the same kind of data on noncertified staff as it does on certified staff, these individuals represent a notable budgetary investment for local school districts. Drawing upon information collected by the New Jersey Education Association, Table 4.4 shows changes in

TABLE 4.4. *Changes in noncertified staff in the*
case study districts, 1990/1993

| | RATIO OF STAFF PER 1000 STUDENTS | | | PERCENT CHANGE |
	1990	1993	CHANGE	IN NUMBER OF STAFF
Secretaries				
Special needs	9.78	10.81	1.03	16%
Transition aid	15.01	10.50	–4.51	–21
Security				
Special needs	2.74	4.03	1.29	55
Transition aid	0.31	0.55	0.24	100
Custodial				
Special needs	13.21	16.00	2.79	27
Transition aid	15.42	11.78	–3.64	–14
Aides				
Special needs	25.68	34.25	8.56	40
Transition aid	15.01	17.35	2.34	30

Note: No data are available on noncertified staff for SN1 and TR4.

these staff categories and the patterns of staffing both before QEA was passed and in 1993 for most of the poor and wealthy districts in the sample. The patterns are different for each category of staff.

With regard to secretaries, the poor urban districts increased available support after the QEA, although this growth was not great. By contrast, just as wealthy districts substantially cut back the number of administrators, they also decreased secretarial support. As a result, while the wealthy districts had about 50% more secretarial support staff per 1,000 students before the QEA began, the ratios were comparable three years later.

Both rich and poor urban districts increased their security forces. In poor districts changes were evenly spread. Most districts had security forces, sometimes with over 100 people. Overall, these forces increased by almost 50%. These increases reflected the changing and increasingly dangerous context of urban New Jersey. One principal explained, "The students in 1971, their presence emanated violence, but there was no violence. Students are now much more violent, and they are apathetic politically, socially, and academically. There are knives, razors, and guns in the school."

The magnitude of the security effort in the wealthy districts was on a totally different scale. In 1990, only one district had any security staff (a total of three in TN3). Three years later, that district had not added security people in spite of substantial growth in the size of the student population, but another district had hired three security people. What is more important, although predictable, is that the poor districts have substantially more security people—nearly 8 times more when considering the size of the student population—than wealthy districts. This is a special cost of doing business in urban areas that wealthy suburban districts do not share.

Another area of staff growth for the poor districts was in custodial and maintenance staff. District SN2 led the growth in maintenance staff. There QEA helped spur a much-needed building program, with its attendant needs for additional and more highly trained staff to operate the more sophisticated systems in newer buildings. Still, growth in this area was quite widespread, reflecting years of deferred maintenance in these districts.

Staff in the special needs districts reported additional wear placed on their facilities by students. One citywide maintenance supervisor described the problems he faced: "I had people in the high school this morning painting over graffiti last night. I had brand new toilets. As soon as you put them in, they are ripped out and thrown through a window. That's life in an urban area."

By contrast, the wealthy districts that were now deferring maintenance, as the poor districts had done in past years, reduced their maintenance staffs. The result was a reversal of staffing patterns over the three years. The transition aid districts had almost a fifth more custodial staff than the special needs districts before the QEA was passed and about a quarter less after three years. While this reduction has long-run implications, the buildings in the wealthy districts were generally newer and in better repair than those in the poor districts, as we detail in Chapter 7, so the short-run problems created were usually more irritating than serious.

Finally, both rich and poor districts increased their use of aides. Part of this was to accommodate the growing special education population in almost all districts. Some districts also incorporated aides into their plans for other programs. SN3, for instance, hired a large number of aides to work in the early childhood programs like full-day kindergarten, and, in keeping with its emphasis on integrating social services, hired a substantial number of aides to serve as liaisons to the community. It made much more extensive use of aides for community relations than any other district.

Overall, the special needs districts used aides much more extensively than did the wealthy ones. In both 1990 and 1993, poor districts had substantially more aides per 1000 students than did wealthy ones. There seemed to be several reasons for this. Although the wealthy and poor districts had about the same proportion of special education students, relatively more of those in poor districts were assigned to regular self-contained classrooms where they required assistance beyond that provided by the regular classroom teacher and where aides are more likely to be assigned. This is just one example of what appears to be a more general pattern of greater reliance upon aides to make up for lower ratios of regular classroom teachers to students in these districts. Thus, special needs districts appear to employ aides to address the special needs of their students and to achieve greater efficiency in the delivery of the regular educational program than they might if they relied solely upon certified teachers.

Distribution of Staff within School Districts

Thus far we have focused on changes in the broad categories of staff employed by local school districts—teachers, administrators, educational services personnel, and various categories of noncertified staff. For a more fine-grained examination of local district staffing patterns, we also explored the assignments of individuals in two of these broad categories, teachers and administrators. Districts deploy teachers and administrators in different ways to meet local needs. Once again, we consider how the patterns of such deployments differ in the special needs and transition aid districts.

TEACHERS

A central issue underlying any effort to use state funding to improve instruction is how teachers are allocated. Table 4.5 provides information on how districts changed their teaching force during the three years after passage of the QEA and the distribution of teachers in 1993 at the end of the 3-year period. This table indicates that in the special needs districts in our case study sample, the percentages of teachers increased in almost every category identified, especially in the art, music, and foreign languages areas. For the most part, SN3 and SN4 made the largest increases, followed by SN6. SN3 made especially large increases in both the art–music–foreign language area, and in special education. The major exception is in business and home economics where a statewide reduction appears underway. Here SN4 broke with the statewide pattern, adding two teachers as part of its effort to increase the availability of electives in the high school, while other districts, including SN3, cut back. In addition, there is essentially no change in the staffing of categorical and vocational programs listed as "Other" in Table 4.5. The overall changes in these six districts are similar to, but more extreme than, patterns of change found in the 30 special needs districts statewide.

The wealthier districts held the line in most areas. In the one area where they cut back—business and home economics—the reductions were substantially larger than in the special needs districts. What appears to be a large increase in the "Other" classification, in fact, represents an increase of 6 teachers to the 42 already working in the vocational and categorical program areas. This growth was primarily in TN2 and also in TN3.

TABLE 4.5. *Assignment of teachers in selected curriculum areas in special needs and transition aid districts in 1993 and percent change from 1990 (case study districts and statewide)*

	CASE STUDY DISTRICTS		STATEWIDE	
CURRICULUM AREAS	TEACHERS/ 1000 STUDENTS IN 1993	PERCENT CHANGE IN NO. OF STAFF	TEACHERS/ 1000 STUDENTS IN 1993	PERCENT CHANGE IN NO. OF STAFF
All				
Special needs	70.65	07%	70.21	05%
Transition aid	67.97	01	72.34	03
Classroom				
Special needs	45.69	01	45.46	05
Transition aid	48.97	01	51.15	03
Art, Music, Foreign Language				
Special needs	4.67	18	4.66	09
Transition aid	8.10	−03	8.23	01
Business, Home Econ.				
Special needs	2.40	−08	2.33	−05
Transition aid	1.53	−25	1.53	−25
Special Education				
Special needs	9.43	11	8.90	09
Transition aid	6.31	11	7.60	11
Other[a]				
Special needs	8.46	01	8.86	00
Transition aid	3.06	14	3.83	−06
Librarians				
Special needs	1.22	04	1.22	05
Transition aid	1.79	08	1.96	01

[a] These are largely teachers of categorical pull-out and vocational programs.

At the end of 3 years, the staffing patterns in the case study districts reflected their different clienteles. The wealthier districts committed more teachers to regular classrooms and to areas of academic and cultural enrichment such as art, music, and foreign languages. The poorer districts had more staff in programs for low-achieving, and non–college-bound students, most notably spe-

cial education, categorical programs, and vocational programs, including business and home economics. Indeed, without the staffing made available by
special programs, students in poor districts would have access to substantially fewer teachers than would students in rich ones. Moreover, these statistics underestimate the teaching hours committed to remedial instruction in particular. In some districts, remedial classes and classes to prepare students
who were likely to have problems passing the state's High School Proficiency
Test (or who already had failed at least once) were assigned to special teachers in ways that were not reported to the state. In other districts, remedial classes
were divided among regular teachers so that work was assigned to teachers
counted in the "classroom teacher" category in Table 4.5.

Administrators

One recurring public debate about educational efficiency focuses on what
has been labeled the "administrative blob." Since Cooper and colleagues (1990)
documented how little money gets to classrooms in New York City schools,
there have been fears that school districts in general, and urban districts in
particular, have too many administrators who contribute little to the production of educational outcomes. New Jersey citizens worried that the QEA funds
would be used to enlarge what they believed were already excessive administrative staffs.

Overall, these fears seem unfounded in both the rich and poor districts
of New Jersey. Statewide, the proportion of certified staff that were administrators was quite small, an identical 8% in both rich and poor districts. Within
our sample, the proportion of administrators was slightly higher in the poor
districts—ranging from a low of 8% to a high of 10%—and slightly lower in
the rich ones, ranging from 6% to 9%. Thus, it is hard to argue that New Jersey's
schools are overstaffed with administrators or that the problem is particularly pervasive in urban districts.

Table 4.6 provides a more detailed picture of the changes in administrative staffs and how administrators were allocated in 1993. Among the special needs districts in our case study sample, there was an 8% increase in the
number of administrators overall. As the breakdown of administrative positions reveals, this increase resulted from a combination of decreases among
central office staff in superintendents' offices, business offices, and those
offices responsible for special students, and from increases among other
central office staff and at the building level where there was a 10% increase
in the number of principals and a 28% increase in the number of assistant
principals. The case study districts differed from the statewide pattern where
there was a very slight reduction in the number of administrators overall.
This reduction was led by a shrinking of central office positions, although
somewhat offset by growth at the building level.

TABLE 4.6. *Changes in selected categories of administrators in special needs and transition aid districts, 1990–1993 (case study districts and statewide)*

ADMINISTRATOR GROUPS	CASE STUDY DISTRICTS		STATEWIDE	
	ADMINS/ 1000 STUDENTS IN 1993	PERCENT CHANGE IN NUMBER OF ADMINS/	ADMIINS/ 1000 STUDENTS IN 1993	PERCENT CHANGE IN NUMBER OF ADMINS.
All				
Special needs	7.13	08%	7.02	–02%
Transition aid	6.57	–25	7.39	–10
Superintendents/Business				
Special needs	0.32	–07	0.40	–06
Transition aid	0.70	00	1.27	–01
Central Office/ Special Students				
Special needs	0.59	–14	0.82	–09
Transition aid	0.26	–33	0.26	–36
Central Office/Other				
Special needs	3.06	05	2.72	–02
Transition aid	3.25	–20	2.94	–17
Principals				
Special needs	1.38	10	1.50	03
Transition aid	1.72	–13	2.00	–03
Assistant Principals				
Special needs	1.78	28	1.57	01
Transition aid	0.29	00	0.92	01

Among the case study districts, there were some notable variations in how changes in the deployment of administrators were made. For instance, SN2 had a net increase of three administrators to bring its staff to 44. The major personnel change was the addition of four vice-principals. It was partly balanced by the loss of one top central office administrator.

By contrast, SN6, a district that increased staff, reduced its administrative cadre by 20% to 82. This district had the reputation of being one of the most poorly administered in the state, and its fiscal operation was under especially close scrutiny by the state during much of the study. Moreover, after a long fight on the school board, the old superintendent was removed, and a new, dynamic top executive was brought in during the study period. The administrative reduction was made primarily in the central office by cutting the very top positions ("superintendents/business" in Table 4.6) in half and reducing lower-level supervisory positions (both "Special Students" and "Other") by 40%.

The transition aid districts experienced a substantial reduction in administrators, and here our sample districts show a statewide phenomenon in accentuated form. Generally, wealthy districts reduced the number of administrators, especially in the lower ranks of the central office staff. Our sample districts followed this pattern but with somewhat deeper cuts, especially at the central office level.

There are important differences in how rich and poor urban districts use administrators. Statewide, the poorer districts assign relatively more administrators to the building level than the central office; 44% of the poor districts' administrators are in buildings as opposed to 40% in wealthy ones. This is something of a surprise given the complaints about the administrative excesses of the poor districts. Special needs districts also have somewhat fewer principals per 1,000 students than the transition aid districts and substantially more assistant principals. These differences probably reflect the larger size of urban schools in general, and particularly the high schools. The poor urban schools may also hire more assistant principals to help maintain order.

Finally, the central office staffs of the wealthy districts are somewhat larger overall on a per-student basis than are those of the poorer districts. This difference may be because almost all the large districts in the state are poor, while the wealthy ones are generally quite small, although there are some small poor districts like SN4. This would explain the greater proportion of top administrators in the small districts, as certain functions must still be performed even for the smaller student bodies. One might expect the poor districts to have large administrative cadres to work with special needs students, either because these districts have so many or as a result of the government regulation that comes with these programs. While these districts do have more administrators for these programs than do wealthier ones (see Central Office/Special Students), the proportion of staff assigned to them turns out to be rather small in the sample districts and also statewide.

CONCLUSIONS

This examination of personnel changes suggests some important conclusions about the extent to which school finance reform in New Jersey contributed to equity between rich and poor districts, the efficiency with which education is delivered (and especially the relative efficiency of rich and poor urban districts), and other factors that mediate the effects of revenue changes on service delivery.

How equal rich and poor districts appear after three years of the QEA depends upon how closely one looks. In broad outline, what stands out is the similarity of the rich and poor districts. Both sets have roughly comparable teacher-student and administrator-student ratios. The inequities between rich and poor districts do not stem from sheer numbers of staff.

Yet these broad outlines hide two important differences. The first is in staff salaries and background. Professionals in wealthy districts are generally paid more than their colleagues in poor districts. A substantial portion of this difference is not attributable to either experience or education. Just working in a poor district generally means getting paid less, especially for administrators. Insofar as financial incentives make a difference in the quality of staff, poor districts are disadvantaged. This financial disadvantage comes on top of the greater propensity to burnout that is typically found in urban districts (see, for example, Dworkin, 1987). Taken together these differences suggest that poor urban districts are less able than wealthy ones to recruit highly talented staff.

In addition, teachers in poor urban districts have less experience than their counterparts in wealthy districts, and staff at all levels have less formal education in poor districts than do those in the same jobs in wealthy districts. While some doubt the value of continuing formal education as it is currently constituted (Murnane, 1995), any advantage in terms of currency of knowledge or intellectual stimulation clearly rests with the wealthy districts.

The other difference is in the allocation of staff. Wealthier districts tend to have more teachers in the academic and cultural enrichment areas of the curriculum (art, music, and foreign language) and more librarians; poor districts have more teachers in special education, vocational, and remedial programs. These differences may be partly a response to the differing clientele of the two sets of districts. Poorer districts do have more profoundly disabled special education students, more students at risk of failing school, and probably more who are vocationally oriented and fewer who will go to college. That is only part of the story, however. As we saw in Chapter 2, the QEA failed to equalize funding for regular education programs. While state and federal categorical aid funds, like special education, Title 1, and at-risk aid, support teachers of special needs students, poor districts simply lack the money to have as many regular classroom teachers, academic specialists, and librarians as wealthier districts.

The personnel data shed some light on the contention that excessive administrative staff might contribute to inefficiency. Although discussion of this issue would benefit from some understanding of what constitutes an "appropriate" number of administrators, the vast majority of the professional staff in New Jersey school districts are clearly teachers. Moreover, the ratios of administrators to students in rich and poor urban districts are roughly comparable; if anything, the wealthier districts are more administratively top heavy than the poor districts. Thus, these data suggest that there is no special inefficiency problem connected to excessive numbers of administrators in poor urban districts.

Finally, changes in staffing seemed to result from a complex mix of financial inputs, salary agreements, and demographic change. The local administrative culture also played a role, but only where other factors combined to create excess resources that could be used to address long-recognized problems.

The first two calls on new funds are the need to meet the existing payroll and fund negotiated raises, and to address enrollment increases. While some researchers dispute the cost effectiveness of small class sizes (Mosteller, 1995; Odden, 1990), allowing growth in class size is unacceptable to both parents and teachers. Only when these needs have been addressed can other issues be confronted. In half our poor urban districts, salaries and population growth absorbed most of the new funding made available by the QEA. Only three districts had the opportunity to add staff above what was required to handle student growth. Two in particular—SN3 and SN4—had aspirations that had lain dormant for years before the QEA provided an opportunity to act on them. These districts moved quickly to implement their visions of improved systems when resources came available. SN6, one of the districts handicapped by internal turmoil, responded less aggressively to the opportunities created by the QEA. It is difficult to know how well this pattern generalizes to the rest of the thirty special needs districts. Still, since both funding and staff growth statewide were lower than in the six sample districts, it is unlikely that many poor urban districts found the resources to add more staff than were needed to respond to population growth.

In the districts where staff did not grow, the kind of reallocation used to start an early childhood program in SN5 was the exception to the rule. In that case, reallocation was facilitated by dynamic leadership combined with some slack resources stemming from administrative layoffs. Even so, this reallocation took place in the context of a significant influx of non–English-speaking students and severe conflict with the city government over the local contribution to school spending.

Meanwhile, the wealthy districts lost staff overall, but this loss reflected a combination of three factors: slow revenue growth, high contract settlements, and—perhaps most important—rapid population growth. Moreover, as noted elsewhere, the slow revenue growth in these districts reflected local taxing decisions more than state policy. Still, many districts, like TN2, may have experienced declining student-staff ratios because enrollment increases overwhelmed new hires.

Where districts did reallocate or cut staff, the rule of thumb was to keep staff close to the students. Thus, central office administrators—especially supervisors and program directors—as well as secretaries and custodial staff, were the first to go. Even with rapid population growth, however, the ratio of classroom teachers; art, music, and foreign language teachers; and librarians to students remained higher in the wealthy districts than in the poor ones. In some cases, however, belt tightening was reducing waste rather than cutting into the bone of educational operations.

In sum, staff changes in both rich and poor districts were driven more by larger demographic, political, and economic forces than any administrative vision of what schools should look like. To see administrators making more discretionary decisions that affected instruction, it is necessary to turn from staffing to changes in curriculum, instruction, and assessment.

5

CURRICULUM, INSTRUCTION, AND ASSESSMENT

The Quality Education Act (QEA) in itself carried no direct implications for general school curricula and instructional practices in New Jersey school districts. The act was a finance reform, not an educational reform. The process spawned by the QEA did require districts receiving additional state funds to engage in systematic program planning as described in Chapter 2, but that planning focused on additional or special programmatic efforts beyond the basic curriculum. However, the QEA was enacted amidst continuing attempts at the national and state levels to bring about a renewal of school curricula and a rethinking of approaches to instruction and assessment. In this chapter we consider how the QEA interacted with these other reform initiatives and the impact on local school district programs. We show that the QEA enabled the poor urban districts to participate in the broader movements for curricular, instructional, and assessment reform in ways not possible in previous years. We also show that, in the end, the urban districts still lag behind their wealthier counterparts in these matters, perhaps because these other districts had sufficient resources to participate in the reforms in the years prior to QEA.

THE BROADER CLIMATE FOR CURRICULUM RENEWAL

Attempts to reform the school curriculum and the instructional practices of teachers have been an enduring part of the history of American education (Kliebard, 1992). The most recent chapter of such reforms can be dated to the 1970s and 1980s, when policy makers and the public at large began questioning whether students were acquiring even the most basic skills necessary to function in the U.S. economic and political systems. This examination of the acquisition of basic skills was accompanied and facilitated by the widespread adoption of competency testing programs at the state level (Anderson & Pipho, 1984). As the discussion in Chapter 2 makes clear, these broader currents of instructional reform have played out in New Jersey as well.

The concern with basic skills acquisition was joined later in the 1980s with a concern about the lack of exposure U.S. students were receiving to core or essential knowledge (Bloom, 1987; Ravitch & Finn, 1987) and to what has been termed *critical thinking* or *higher order skills* (Fry, 1992). The interest in higher order thinking skills has pervaded discussions of new curricular, instructional, and assessment approaches in the areas of literacy and mathematics, among others.

In language arts, the earlier concern with basic literacy skills reflected in the skills-based curricula, the back-to-basics instructional strategies, and the minimal competency testing programs of the seventies and eighties has been joined by concern about the development of students as literate thinkers, individuals who can not only read and write correctly, but who can also reason about what they are learning. The emphasis on higher order thinking and learning is reflected in more-demanding curricular material, social constructivist approaches to instruction, and assessments that are more holistic and performance based. Along these lines, recent theory and research (Langer & Allington, 1992) suggest that the classroom is a social community, with characteristic ways of reading, writing, and thinking, and that language arts learning should occur in ways appropriate to that community.

Reform efforts in mathematics curriculum, instruction, and assessment have also grown substantially in recent years. The emphasis on basic mathematical skills that emerged in the seventies and early eighties has given way to new conceptualizations of mathematics instruction. This movement has been driven principally by the mathematics standards developed by the National Council of Teachers of Mathematics (1989). The approach includes a curriculum characterized by a broad range of content, contexts, and deliberate connections; instruction that encourages active participation, communication, and reasoning about real problems; and assessment that is performance based and directed toward facilitating learning (Romberg, 1992).

An important aspect of the most recent approaches to curriculum, instruction, and assessment is the assumption that all students can learn and should be exposed to challenging material. Concerns have been raised from a number of perspectives regarding the access to knowledge afforded students from different groups in U.S. society. Of course, there has long been a concern that poor and minority students have limited access to valued knowledge (Bourdieu & Passeron, 1990; Bowles & Gintis, 1976). Differential access has been seen to be a problem at all organizational levels: within the classroom (Slavin & Braddock, 1993), between classrooms and tracks (Oakes, 1995), and between schools and districts (Orfield, 1994a). In addition to removing the structural barriers to knowledge that impede the progress of certain groups of students, current approaches to curriculum reform include the expansion of the curriculum to encompass materials that might engage students from minority cultural groups (Banks, 1993).

The most appropriate instructional approach for at-risk students has been the subject of some contention. Although some researchers have advocated the use of the less-directive strategies generally associated with progressive education and constructivist approaches, others have suggested that when such strategies are followed to the exclusion of more skill-oriented approaches, the learning of at-risk students is impeded (Delpit, 1995). Following a review of the systematic evaluations of various instructional programs, Natriello et al. (1990) concluded that the most effective programs for enhancing the learning of at-risk students adjusted instruction to the needs of individual students while maximizing academically focused, teacher-directed activities involving sequenced and structured approaches. Thus, the combination of a traditional skills-based approach with more challenging higher order thinking and reasoning may offer students at risk of school failure, such as many of those in the special needs districts, the greatest opportunity to succeed.

In this chapter we show that this blend of skills-based instruction with added attention to constructivist approaches and higher order skills seems to characterize the poor urban districts in New Jersey in the wake of QEA. In fact, most urban districts in our case studies reported using the additional funds available under QEA to move their language arts and mathematics programs in the direction suggested by the curriculum reform movement and supported by the state in the wake of the *Abbott* decision as encouraged by the court.

THE NEW JERSEY CONTEXT FOR CURRICULUM REFORM

The current curriculum reform movement provides the larger context for examining developments in the educational programs of special needs districts, foundation aid districts, and transition aid districts in New Jersey in the wake of the QEA. However, there is also a context more directly related to New Jersey school districts. In Chapter 2 we recounted many of the dimensions of this more local context, some of which grew out of the QEA and some of which stemmed from ongoing reform efforts in the state.

Thus far we have not considered directly the implications of the *Abbott v Burke* decision for the educational programs of local districts, but this case also has important implications for any analysis of the shape and substance of curriculum, instruction, and assessment in New Jersey schools. In *Abbott* the court offered a discussion of curriculum and instruction issues that parallels discussions about basic skills and higher order tasks among contemporary curriculum reformers. After reviewing educational programs in wealthy and poor school districts in New Jersey, the court concluded that "many of these poorer urban districts are burdened with teaching basic skills to an overwhelming number of students. They are essentially "basic skills districts"" (*Abbott v Burke* 1990, p. 362).

The court went on to reject basic skills as meeting the constitutional requirement of providing a "thorough and efficient" education:

> Thorough and efficient means more than teaching the skills needed to compete in the labor market, as critically important as that may be. It means being able to fulfill one's role as a citizen, a role that encompasses far more than merely registering to vote. It means the ability to participate fully in society, in the life of one's community, the ability to appreciate music, art, and literature, and the ability to share all of that with friends. (pp. 363–364)

The court further contrasted the basic skills instruction that characterized the poor urban districts with the more diverse and challenging offerings of the wealthy districts:

> Alongside these basic-skills districts are school systems offering the broadest range of courses, instruction in numerous languages, sophisticated mathematics, arts, and sciences at a high level, fully equipped laboratories, hands-on computer experience, everything parents seriously concerned for their children's future would want, and everything a child needs. (p. 364)

The court continued by reviewing the state's argument that basic skills instruction is most appropriate for the students in the poorer districts:

> The State contends that the education currently offered in these poorer urban districts is tailored to the students' present need, that these students simply cannot now benefit from the kind of vastly superior course offerings found in the richer districts. No one claims here, however, that students unable to attain a level of reading, writing, or expression even approaching the expectations of their grade, pupils who according to plaintiffs, are 2 years behind others on the first day they enter school, would be able to take full advantage of the richness of course offerings found in the wealthier suburbs. The State's conclusion is that basic skills are what they need first, intensive training in basic skills. (p. 364)

The court rejected the state's position on this issue:

We note, however, that these poorer districts offer curricula denuded not only of advanced academic courses but of virtually every subject that ties a child, particularly a child with academic problems, to school—of art, music, drama, athletics, even to a very substantial degree, of science and social studies. The result violates not only our sense of what constitutes a thorough and efficient education, but the statute as well, which requires "(a) breadth of program offerings designed to develop the individual talents and abilities of students." *N.J.S.A.* 18A:7A–5d. However articulated, such a requirement must encompass more than "instruction . . . in the basic communications and computational skills," which the statute cites as another major element in education. *N.J.S.A.* 18:7A–5c. (pp. 364–365)

The court concluded by recommending an educational program that would encompass both basic skills and the higher order tasks advocated by curriculum reformers:

In saying this we disparage neither these districts' decision to focus on remedial training, nor the State testing requirements that may have prompted this focus. But constitutionally, these districts should not be limited to such choices. However, desperately, a child may need remediation in basic skills, he or she also needs at least a modicum of variety and a chance to excel. (pp. 365–366)

In a footnote at this point the court even suggested the potential value of the constructivist approach to curriculum and instruction appearing in the research literature:

Beyond this, recent scholarly discussion has focused heavily on the need for individualized instruction tailored to children's different needs and development patterns, experiential learning—ranging from scientific experiments to poetry writing—that responds to and develops children's curiosity, and interventions that address the hostile attitudes minority children may bring to a system often perceived as "white" and alien. Much of this research suggests that schools may fail to build on the knowledge and skills poor and minority children bring to school, strengths often different from those of white, middle class children of the same age. . . . As judges rather than educators or social scientists, we are in no position to assess the value of these approaches or the place they should be given relative to more traditional book and workbook exercises. Nevertheless, it seems clear to us that experimentation is needed to reverse the staggering failure of our poorer urban districts, and that experimentation itself requires money. (note, p. 366)

The court decision thus articulated a view of curriculum that includes both basic skills and more-demanding higher order tasks in a constructivist approach that takes into account the backgrounds and conditions of the students. Moreover, the court proposed that additional resources would allow such approaches to be tried in New Jersey's poor urban districts. Our analysis of the impact of the QEA on curriculum, instruction, and assessment in local school districts examined this proposition and, as we will demonstrate, found most of our urban case study districts using QEA funds to accomplish precisely what the court proposed: a curriculum that included, but moved beyond, basic skills. Before examining the educational programs in local districts along these dimensions, we first consider the extent to which state and local forces influence local districts.

INFLUENCES ON LOCAL DISTRICTS: DIFFERENTIAL EFFECTS

In the early 1990s New Jersey school districts were dealing not only with the changes in school finance represented in the QEA, but also with several state policies designed to shape local approaches to curriculum and instruction. The later policies discussed in Chapter 2, together with developments at the national level discussed above, influenced the ways in which New Jersey school districts attempted to shape their approaches to the curriculum, classroom instruction, and assessment.

By the early 1990s the state had been engaged in activities to influence curriculum, instruction, and assessment in school districts for several years. To assess the impact of such state actions on the three types of school districts, in the 1993 district survey, superintendents were asked to rate the influence of various groups and entities on the content of their educational programs on a 5-point scale ranging from 1 for "Not at all influential" to 5 for "Extremely influential." Local school boards were rated as the most influential (4.54), followed by central office personnel (4.30), and school-based administrators (4.27). The state government was the next most influential entity (3.53), far ahead of federal government (2.01) and city government (1.67). Thus, in the early 1990s the state government was the most influential force on the school curriculum outside of the immediate district.

Two specific state policies offer a more concrete portrait of state influence in different kinds of districts. As noted in Chapter 2, New Jersey operated a program for monitoring school districts in the 1980s. Monitoring examined a wide range of district operating characteristics, including the curriculum. State monitoring of special needs districts involved additional scrutiny by the Division of Urban Education (DUE) as part of the QEA. When district administrators statewide were asked to rate the influence of state monitoring on the content of their programs in the 1993 district survey on a scale ranging from 1 (Not at all influential) to 5 (Extremely influential), they rated state monitoring activities very influential (3.61). Not surprisingly, administrators in special needs districts rated the influence of state monitoring as higher (3.91) than administrators in foundation aid districts (3.72) and those in transition aid districts (3.46), though these differences were not statistically significant.

The state competency testing program offers another more specific state policy to assess for its impact on local district programs. As noted in Chapter 2 the state has had a minimum competency testing program in place since 1978. These basic skills tests in reading, writing, and mathematics had caused many districts to redirect their curricula. In the 1993 district survey, administrators rated the competency testing program as very influential (3.79) over the content of the district curriculum.

Since the testing program had proven more of a challenge for special needs districts than for others, it is not surprising that administrators in those districts rated the testing program as more influential (4.33) than administrators in foundation aid districts (3.94) and those in transition aid districts (3.60). These ratings were significantly different ($F = 3.19; p < .05$).

Beginning in the 1993/94 school year, districts had to contend with a new more demanding high school proficiency test required for graduation first administered in the eleventh grade as well as a challenging early warning test administered in the eighth grade. While the original high school proficiency test caused local educators to redouble their efforts at basic skills instruction, the new, more demanding tests drove them to seek curriculum and instruction that encompassed higher order thinking and problem-solving skills.

Although all local districts are susceptible to state influence, the statewide survey data make it clear that this influence does not always fall with the same impact on different kinds of districts. Special needs districts, those that receive the most support from state sources, are sometimes, as in the case of the state testing program, subject to greater state influence. This is in contrast to popular views of urban districts that portray them as isolated and beyond the control of state authorities. In the sections that follow, we consider some specific results of state influence in the aftermath of the QEA.

CURRICULUM, INSTRUCTION, AND ASSESSMENT

Policies designed to shape local district approaches to curriculum, instruction, and assessment were separate from the QEA and, in fact, predated it. They created the environment of concern into which the additional funds associated with the QEA entered in 1991. To clarify the impact of the QEA and other state policies on the curriculum, instruction, and assessment practices of New Jersey school districts, we examine the major patterns evident in the early 1990s. We pay particular attention to changes along the dimensions identified in the professional literature as promising avenues for renewal. We focus our inquiry on language arts and mathematics both because these areas are central to the core academic program and because they have been the subject of substantial rethinking in recent years. Each of these areas offers insight into how different kinds of districts modified their practices during the period of time when the QEA was implemented.

To understand changes in the regular programs of the special needs, foundation aid, and transition aid districts, we brought together several sources of data. First, we used data from our interviews with superintendents and curriculum directors at the central offices as well as from our interviews with principals, teachers, and guidance staff at individual schools. Second, we analyzed curriculum materials collected at both the district and school levels. Third, we drew on our surveys of teachers in the case study districts. Fourth, we examined selected items from our two statewide surveys of superintendents.

In our interviews respondents in the special needs districts reported that the QEA has enabled them to engage fully in curriculum development activities for the first time. As respondents noted, the early nineties marked the first time in memory that special needs districts could adopt new textbook series in all their grade levels instead of phasing in purchases one grade level at a time. Respondents also noted that they were able to purchase the ancillary materials that publishers prepare to go with textbook series.

We found specific instances of these trends in a number of our interviews. In district SN2, for example, the math coordinator reported that the district curriculum was realigned to be consistent with NCTM standards "away from computation and rote memory to problem solving, connections, and communications." To accomplish this, new funds were used to purchase new text series, to send teachers to workshops, and to acquire sets of graphing calculators for all classes in grades 7 through 12. Additional funds were used to ensure that students had access to computers with appropriate math software, as well as tools and manipulatives. The coordinator then showed the interviewer a closet full of math manipulatives, games, and other learning aids ready to be sent to the schools. Resources were also used to support extracurricular activities that build on the new curriculum. As the coordinator noted, "Last weekend we sent 24 kids to Boston for Boston University's Peak Performance competition where they had to build cars to go to the top of a hill and stay there. We took 5 out of the top 22 positions; our best finish was a third place." In this district QEA resources clearly enabled a full-press reform of the math program along the lines suggested by the curriculum reformers.

This pattern of more readily available curriculum resources in the special needs districts among our case study districts was confirmed in the 1993 statewide survey of districts. In that survey superintendents were asked to describe their spending on textbooks and on equipment as increasing, remaining stable, or decreasing. Over three-fourths (76.5%) of the special needs districts reported increased spending on equipment, and nearly two-thirds (64.7%) reported increased spending on textbooks. No special needs districts reported decreased spending on equipment or textbooks. Among foundation aid districts, about half (49.6%) reported increased spending on equipment, and just under that (48.8%) reported increased spending on textbooks; 35.2% reported stable spending and 15.2% reported declining spending on equipment; and 44.8% reported stable spending and 6.4% reported declining spending on textbooks. Among transition aid districts 44.2% reported increased equipment spending, and 43.0% reported increased textbook spending; 36.4% reported stable spending on equipment and 51.7% reported stable spending on textbooks; and 19.5% reported declining spending on equipment, while 5.3% reported declining spending on textbooks.

Several special needs districts among those in our case studies engaged in new spending for staff development to support curriculum renewal. This pattern was borne out in our survey data as well. Among special needs districts, 76.5% reported increasing the number of teachers served by staff development compared to 62.4% of foundation aid districts and 71.4% of transition aid districts. Of special needs districts, 17.6% held the number of teachers involved in staff development stable, compared to 34.4% of foundation aid districts and 22.1% of transition aid districts. Small proportions of special needs districts (5.9%), foundation aid districts (3.2%), and transition aid districts (6.5%) reported declines in the number of teachers served by staff development.

The general picture that emerges from this statewide survey is that special needs districts were more likely than other districts to increase spending on textbooks, equipment, and staff development in the wake of the QEA. These investments support curriculum development and renewal. The pattern of increases among special needs districts suggests that they were in a better position to support curriculum development than in the recent past.

However, even with the improvements in the ability to purchase curriculum materials in the special needs districts, teachers in these districts still rated the availability of texts as less adequate than did teachers in either foundation aid or transition aid districts (see Table 5.1). The second column in the table shows the mean teacher responses in eleven of our 12 case study districts. Teachers were asked to rate the adequacy of texts on a scale ranging from 1 ("Very inadequate") to 4 ("Very adequate"). The mean teacher responses in the special needs districts ranged from 2.69 in SN3 to 3.04 in SN2. Responses in the foundation aid districts were 3.04 in FN2 and 3.20 in FN1. Responses in the transition aid districts ranged from 3.12 in TR4 to 3.44 in TR1. Teachers' ratings were significantly higher in transition aid districts than in special needs districts, with the foundation aid districts in between.

TABLE 5.1. *Mean teacher ratings of the adequacy of textbooks and computer resources by district, 1992*

| | TEXTBOOKS | | COMPUTER RESOURCES | |
DISTRICT	MEAN	N	MEAN	N
SN1	2.87	203	2.07	144
SN2	3.04	193	2.17	152
SN3	2.69	281	1.89	231
SN4	2.89	168	1.71	143
SN5	2.90	306	2.02	201
FN1	3.20	127	2.28	114
FN2	3.04	167	2.36	157
TR1	3.44	173	2.32	158
TR2	3.43	100	2.90	105
TR3	3.16	127	2.67	127
TR4	3.12	118	2.78	116
SN	2.87[a]	1,151	1.97[b]	871
FN	3.10	294	2.32	271
TR	3.30	518	2.63	506
All districts	3.02	1,963	2.23	1,648

Responses: 1 = very inadequate, 2 = somewhat inadequate, 3 = adequate, 4 = very adequate.
[a] $F = 21.28, p < .001$
[b] $F = 69.52, p < .001$

The fourth column of Table 5.1 displays the mean teacher adequacy ratings of computer resources in eleven of our 12 case study districts in 1992. The five lowest ratings are in the special needs districts, ranging from 1.71 in SN4 to 2.17 in SN2. The two foundation aid districts have ratings of 2.36 in FN2 and 2.28 in FN1. The four transition aid districts have ratings ranging from 2.32 in TR1 to 2.9 in TR2.

These 1992 data no doubt reflect differences in patterns of resource distribution not yet affected by QEA funds. However, additional data from both the 1992 and 1994 teacher surveys confirm that, despite the increased availability of resources for curriculum and instruction in the special needs districts, these districts were still less well off than the foundation aid districts or the transition aid districts. In 1992 teachers were asked to rate the adequacy of textbooks, computers; notebooks and paper, pens and pencils; reusable material such as equipment and calculators; and nonreusable material such as wookbooks and practice sheets. In 1994 teachers were asked to rate the adequacy of these items plus library books, manipulative materials, supplemental reading and research materials, and nontext materials such as audiotapes, records, CD-ROMs and videos or laser disks. In each case in each year the mean responses for special needs district teachers were lower than the mean teacher responses for the other two groups; the mean teacher responses for teachers in the transition aid districts were higher than those of teachers in either the special needs districts or the foundation aid districts. The persistence of this pattern during the early 1990s suggests that, despite the improvements associated with the QEA, the relative standing of the three kinds of districts in terms of materials for curriculum and instruction remained the same.

Overall, there are two patterns in both our case study and survey data. First, the special needs districts used the resources provided through the QEA to enhance their general program of curriculum and instruction. Second, the relatively weaker position of the special needs districts in these areas continued, despite the additional resources. In the remainder of this chapter we examine the more particular patterns of changes in language arts and math in our case study districts and in districts throughout the state.

Language Arts

As noted earlier, there have been proposals from a variety of quarters to reform language arts curriculum, instructional approaches, and assessment strategies. We consider each of these in turn as they affected language arts in our 12 case study districts. Of course, since these three areas tend to interact, our discussion of each often includes references to the others.

Across our case study districts, we find considerable uncertainty about movement toward constructivism or whole language and away from basic skills. Rather, districts appear to be forging blends of constructivist and skills-based approaches. Nevertheless, the transition aid districts are adopting constructivist practices somewhat more quickly and thoroughly than their special needs counterparts.

LANGUAGE ARTS CURRICULUM

Only one special needs district appears to be embracing this movement fully, with a "holistic, integrated, literature-based" program (SN4). Three other special needs districts have expanded their curricula to include constructivist and applied strategies but have held on to such traditional basic skills teaching practices as textbooks, grammar books, and decoding strategies (SN3, SN5, SN2). In the final two special needs districts (SN1, SN6), much of the curricular uncertainty reflects lack of coordination throughout the district and related difficulties in mobilizing the teaching staffs. For all these districts, particularly the five that have shifted more slowly, the overriding concern is that the new state High School Proficiency Test (HSPT) is not strictly constructivist or applied. These districts are hesitant to risk test scores by trying an entirely new approach.

Among the non–special needs districts, one district has fully embraced the whole language approach. This district no longer purchases textbooks or workbooks for kindergarten through eighth grade (TR1). No other non–special needs district has pursued constructivism with equal vigor; however, two other districts (TR2, TR4) have progressively added constructivist elements to their curricula over the past 5 years. Another district (FN1) revised its curriculum to include these elements, but it was just starting in the fall of 1994. The last two (TR3, FN2) remain the most conservative; while they bought products to support constructivist approaches, administrators and teachers approach change quite hesitantly.

One early indicator of a district's commitment to curriculum change is the provision of relevant staff development opportunities. When elementary teachers were asked on the 1994 teacher survey to indicate whether they had received in-service staff development in whole language instruction in the past 3 years, the differences by district type were not significant. However, Table 5.2 reveals substantial differences across individual districts.

These teacher reports clearly show that SN4, FN1, and TR2 engaged in the broadest staff development effort around the whole language approach to language arts instruction. While at least some teachers in all districts had been exposed to staff development related to whole language instruction, over 60% of the teachers surveyed in these districts had received some staff development of this nature. Other districts, notably SN1, FN2, and TR4, appear to lag substantially in this regard with proportions of teachers receiving staff development in whole language half or less of those in SN4.

A more direct indication of the variety of district approaches to language arts curriculum comes from a question on the 1994 teacher survey pertaining to major approaches to English and language arts in the case study school districts. Teachers were asked to indicate what English/language arts represented in their school and were given three choices representing different conceptions of the field:

> English/language arts is primarily a set of skills defined by clear rules that allow you to reach satisfactory outcomes.
> English/language arts is primarily a process that permits you to clarify your ideas.
> English/language arts is primarily a way of communicating your ideas to others.

TABLE 5.2. *Proportions of elementary teachers in the case study districts who reported receiving staff development in whole language instruction between 1991/92 and 1993/94*

DISTRICT	PROPORTIONS	NO. OF RESPONSES
SN1	.22	79
SN2	.58	64
SN3	.59	160
SN4	.91	55
SN5	.59	220
SN6	.46	50
FN1	.75	36
FN2	.42	45
TR1	—[a]	—
TR2	.63	46
TR3	.49	68
TR4	.38	96
SN	.56[b]	628
FN	.57	81
TR	.47	210
All districts	.54	919

[a] No elementary teachers in TR1 completed the survey.
[b] $F = 2.77, p < .10$

The first conception, English as a set of skills, is the most traditional view of the field. The second conception, focusing on the clarification of ideas, exemplifies a more constructivist approach. The third conception, emphasizing communications, takes a more applied approach. There were substantial differences in the patterns of teacher responses by district type. Teachers in all three types of districts were most likely to report that English/language arts is primarily a way of communicating ideas to others; however, the actual percentages differed with 45.2% of teachers in special needs districts, 56.1% of teachers in foundation aid districts, and 61.5% of teachers in transition aid districts selecting this option. The perspective that English/language arts is a process to clarify ideas was chosen by 19.8% of the teachers in transition aid districts, 16.7% of foundation aid district teachers, and only 11.6% of special needs district teachers. In the special needs districts nearly as many teachers (43.2%) treated English/language arts as a set of skills defined by clear rules as those who considered it a way of communicating. Substantially fewer teachers in the foundation aid districts (27.2%) and in the transition aid districts (18.7%) viewed English/language arts as a set of skills. Thus, teachers in the special needs districts were the most likely to hold traditional views on English/language arts.

Differences are also apparent at the individual district level as indicated in Figure 5.1. The special needs district with the lowest proportion of teachers reporting that English/language arts is primarily a set of skills is SN5 with one-third of teachers indicating the skills-based approach; in all other special needs districts considerably higher proportions of teachers indicate the skills-based approach. Only one non–special needs district (FN2) comes close to having as high a proportion of teachers choosing the skills-based approach;

FIGURE 5.1. *Proportions of teachers indicating the primary conception of English/language arts in their school*

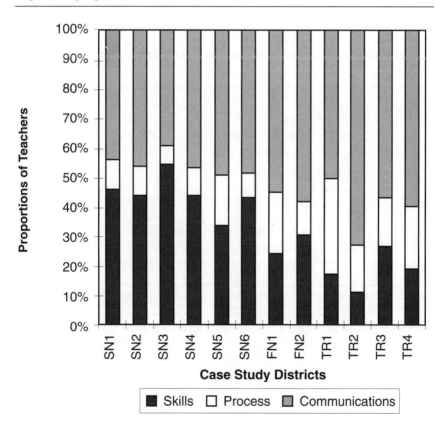

most non–special needs districts have considerably fewer than one-third of their teachers indicating that skills dominate language arts instruction in their schools. Thus, although all of our 12 districts have substantial proportions of teachers describing their English and language arts program as other than skills based, the six special needs districts maintain the most traditional approach to this area of the curriculum.

Multiculturalism has also been suggested as a way to improve language arts education, particularly for minority students. Although districts vary on what they categorize as *multicultural*, almost all districts, with the exception of two (TR3, FN2), are making at least some attempt to enrich their curricula with literature or other representations of culture from other nations/heritages. However, note that the two exceptions are not among the special needs districts. All the special needs districts are giving, at minimum, moderate attention to multicultural issues and, at maximum, have made major commitments to multiculturalism in language arts.

Another issue that arose from our observations in the districts was the extent of district-to-school consistency in curriculum. Four special needs districts seem to have centralized processes for making decisions regarding curriculum that result in substantial consistency among schools (SN2, SN3, SN4, SN5). In one (SN3), however, some schools seem to be moving even faster than the central office. In another (SN5), although the schools align with the central office, all seem torn over the proper direction for their curriculum. The two other special needs districts (SN1, SN6) have little alignment between the district office and the schools. However, some individual schools in these districts have tried to update and improve their curricula.

The non–special needs districts tend to be less centralized than the special needs districts. However, two districts (FN2, TR1) seem to be well articulated across all 12 grades, even though one is still debating the proper direction of its curriculum. In one other district (FN1), the elementary and middle schools are well aligned with the central office, but the high school lags behind considerably. None of the three other non–special needs districts have much in terms of centralizing curriculum personnel; therefore, individuals in the schools tend to drive the curriculum without much systematic input from above.

All 12 districts appear much more willing to move toward new approaches to curriculum at the early grades than at the high school level. Our case study interviews suggested that the high school curriculum in each district was the least likely to embrace the current thinking about curriculum reform.

Finally, all districts do some tracking. The number of tracks ranges from two to five segments of the student body, and most districts have either three or four, regardless of district type. Special needs districts tend to have larger tracks (i.e., more sections) directed to lower achieving students, while transition aid districts tend to have larger tracks directed to higher achieving students.

INSTRUCTION IN LANGUAGE ARTS

Teachers' instructional activities have also been the focus of attempts to reform work in English and language arts. Although many instructional issues have been raised, we consider only those that surfaced in our case study interviews or were examined in one of the teacher surveys.

One question on the 1994 teacher survey focuses on the use of traditional approaches to instruction in language arts. Teachers were asked to report on how frequently they asked students to do something quite traditional in language arts: work on a workbook, worksheet, or on questions at the end of a chapter. There were significant differences across the three types of districts ($F = 17.8$, $p < .001$), with teachers in special needs districts reporting such traditional assignments more frequently (3.20) than teachers in foundation aid districts (3.12) and those in transition aid districts (2.72; see Table 5.3).

The second column of Table 5.3 shows the mean responses of teachers to this item for each case study district. Teachers in all the special needs districts still appear to rely on these traditional classroom tasks. This is so even in SN4 where there has been a serious commitment to the whole language approach. By contrast, teachers in TR1, the transition aid district with the greatest commitment to the whole language approach, report infrequent use of these traditional tasks. The whole language approach may have been added to the traditional approach in the special needs districts, while at least in a few transition aid districts it may be displacing the traditional approach.

The constructivist movement in English and language arts emphasizes much more writing than absolutist methods of teaching. Writing instruction includes practices such as journal keeping and teaching the writing process. Our case study interviews suggest that most of the 12 districts have increased the amount of writing in their language arts programs, and the differences between districts do not fall along district type lines. Only one special needs district (SN1) and one wealthy district (TR3) stand out as relatively low in their emphasis on writing compared to the other ten districts.

Data from the teacher survey also focus on the issue of the amount of writing instruction. Teachers reported how frequently students were asked to write about their reading, how often students were asked to write in a journal, how often teachers devoted attention to the stages of the writing process, how often they devoted attention to the technical aspects and skills of writing, and how often they had students write in styles that encourage their emotional and imaginative development. There were no significant differences by district type in terms of the frequency with which students were asked to write in a journal, the frequency of teacher attention to the stages of the writing process, and the frequency with which teachers devoted attention to the technical aspects of writing. In these areas the reports from the teachers in the three types of districts were similar. There were differences in the frequency with which

TABLE 5.3. *Mean teacher responses regarding the frequency of the use of workbooks/worksheets/end of chapter questions and group work in language arts instruction by district*

| DISTRICT | WORKBOOKS/SHEETS/QUESTIONS | | GROUP WORK | |
	MEAN	N	MEAN	N
SN1	3.34	73	1.96	67
SN2	3.22	93	2.21	89
SN3	3.37	122	2.44	99
SN4	3.02	85	2.15	82
SN5	3.16	167	2.46	164
SN6	2.96	51	2.02	45
FN1	3.14	37	2.31	48
FN2	3.11	53	2.44	45
TR1	1.33	12	2.33	6
TR2	2.34	32	2.43	37
TR3	3.16	58	2.36	50
TR4	2.77	57	2.64	61
SN	3.20[a]	591	2.27[B]	546
FN	3.12	90	2.38	93
TR	2.72	159	2.49	154
All districts	3.10	840	2.33	793

Responses: 1 = never or hardly ever, 2 = once or twice a month, 3 = once or twice a week, 4 = almost every day.
[a] $F = 17.8, p < .001$
[b] $F = 4.04, p < .05$

students were asked to write about their reading ($F = 3.37, p < .05$), with teachers in transition aid districts reporting this activity most frequently (3.22), following by teachers in special needs districts (3.09), and teachers in foundation aid districts (2.99). There were also significant differences by district type in how frequently students were asked to write in styles to encourage their emotional and imaginative development ($F = 3.57, p < .05$), with teachers in the transition aid districts indicating the highest frequency of such activity (3.04), followed by teachers in the foundation aid districts (2.91), and those in the special needs districts (2.83).

Another element that has been advocated as a technique for improving language arts instruction is cooperative learning (Slavin, 1991). A question on the teacher survey asked teachers to report on how frequently students did group work in English/language arts. Possible responses ranged from 1 ("Never or hardly ever") to 2 ("Once or twice a month"), to 3 ("Once or twice a week"), to 4 ("Almost every day"). The analysis of variance results indicated that there were significant differences by district type ($F = 4.04$, $p < .018$) with teachers in transition aid districts reporting the most frequent group work (2.49), followed by teachers in foundation aid districts (2.38), and those in special needs districts (2.27).

The fourth column of Table 5.3 shows the mean teacher responses to this question regarding group work in each of our 12 case study districts. Group activities do not dominate in any district. The mean teacher responses in most of the districts indicate that such group work occurs somewhere between "Once or twice a month" and "Once or twice a week." Among the special needs districts teachers in SN1, SN4, and SN6 report the least frequent use of group work, while those in SN3 and SN5 report the most frequent use. In only one non–special needs district (TR4) do teachers report more frequent use of group work in language arts than in SN5.

Along with the inclusion of multicultural elements in the school curriculum, some researchers have also advocated greater attention to developing instructional strategies to help teachers respond to the needs of students from different backgrounds. An item on the 1994 teacher survey asked teachers to report whether they had received staff development on teaching students from different cultural backgrounds in the past 3 years. An analysis of variance revealed significant differences in teacher replies by district type ($F = 7.08$, $p < .001$), with teachers in special needs districts being more likely to report such activity in the past 3 years (38.6%), followed by teachers in both the foundation aid districts (26.1%) and transition aid districts (26.1%; see Table 5.4). The second column of Table 5.4 shows the variation within the three district types by district.

These reports from the teacher survey are consistent with those obtained in our site visit interviews: TR3 and FN2 are the two districts with the smallest proportions of teachers reporting staff development on teaching students from different cultures in the past 3 years. Although teachers in special needs districts are significantly more likely to report receiving such in-service training, there is substantial variation within the district types: in special needs districts the range is from SN4 with 26% of teachers reporting such training to SN3 where 47% of the teachers report receiving training in diversity; in foundation aid districts 9% of teachers in FN2 and 46% of teachers in FN1 report receiving diversity training; in the transition aid districts 12% of the teachers in TR3 and 60% of the teachers in TR2 report receiving diversity training.

TABLE 5.4. *Proportions of teachers reporting receiving*
in-service staff development in teaching students from different
cultural backgrounds and in teaching reading and writing across
the curriculum between 1991/92 and 1993/94 school years, by district

| DISTRICT | DIVERSE BACKGROUNDS | | READ/WRIT ACROSS CURRICULUM | |
	MEAN	N	MEAN	N
SN1	.41	164	.27	164
SN2	.35	218	.37	218
SN3	.47	272	.38	272
SN4	.26	189	.42	189
SN5	.41	362	.56	362
SN6	.34	121	.31	121
FN1	.46	109	.51	109
FN2	.09	125	.31	125
TR1	.48	46	.61	46
TR2	.60	93	.31	93
TR3	.12	116	.45	116
TR4	.33	179	.32	179
SN	.39[a]	1,326	.41[b]	1,326
FN	.26	234	.41	234
TR	.26	434	.38	434
All districts	.36	1,994	.41	1,994

[a] $F = 7.08, p < .001$
[b] $F = .67$, NS

A final indicator of movement in language arts education is the extent to which there is integration of various subjects across the curriculum. An item on the 1994 teacher survey asked teachers to report on whether they had received staff development in the past 3 years in teaching reading and writing across the curriculum. There were no significant differences among teachers in the three district types. However, there are some substantial differences among individual districts in the proportions of teachers exposed to such in-service training in the past 3 years. The fourth column of Table 5.4 shows the proportions of teachers in our case study districts reporting that they received such training. The three districts with the highest proportions of teachers reporting that they had received staff development in teaching reading and writing across the curriculum are TR1, SN5, and FN1; the three lowest are SN1, SN6, and TR2. These patterns appear to be related to individual district commitments, not to district types.

Although all 12 districts are moving ahead with new approaches to instruction to some extent, the special needs districts are lagging behind in several respects. Teachers in the special needs districts were most likely to report using traditional assignments in English and language arts, least likely to utilize writing assignments that encourage emotional and imaginative development in students, least likely to engage in group work, and least likely to have received training in reading and writing across the curriculum. Teachers in special needs districts were most likely to report receiving in-service training in responding to the needs of diverse learners.

ASSESSMENT IN ENGLISH/LANGUAGE ARTS

Assessment is a third major area in which there have been calls for reform in recent years (Airasian, 1991; Berlak et al., 1992; Wiggins, 1993). The movement of all districts away from the traditional approach to English/language arts as solely skills based and the slight lag in this movement on the part of special needs districts are illustrated in teacher responses to several questions pertaining to assessment in English and language arts on the 1994 teacher survey.

One item on the survey asked teachers to choose either mechanical correctness or the communication of ideas as the most important criterion for evaluating student performance in English/language arts. A large majority of teachers in all three types of districts selected the communication of ideas as the most important criterion. However, the special needs districts lagged slightly behind the foundation and transition aid districts in this regard. In special needs districts 87.1% of the teachers selected the communication of ideas versus 12.9% who selected mechanical correctness. The corresponding figures in the foundation aid districts were 94.1% and 5.9%; in transition aid districts the figures were 97.6% and 2.4%. There were significant differences by district type ($F = 9.03$, $p < .001$). Thus while the vast majority of teachers in all three types of districts selected the communication of ideas as the most important criterion, the proportion of respondents selecting this criterion was highest in the transition aid districts and lowest in the special needs districts.

Figure 5.2 shows the teacher responses to this question by district. In five of the six special needs districts (SN1, SN2, SN3, SN4, SN5) at least 10% of the teachers reported that mechanical correctness was the most important criterion in evaluating student work in English and language arts; in SN6, only 6.1% of the teachers selected mechanical correctness. In five of the six non–special needs districts (FN2, TR1, TR2, TR3, TR4), fewer than 4% of the teachers selected mechanical correctness; in FN1, 8.5% of the teachers indicated that mechanical correctness was the most important criterion in evaluating student work in English and language arts. The vast majority of teachers in all

FIGURE 5.2. *Proportions of teachers indicating mechanical correctness and communication of ideas as the most important criterion for evaluating student performance in English/language arts*

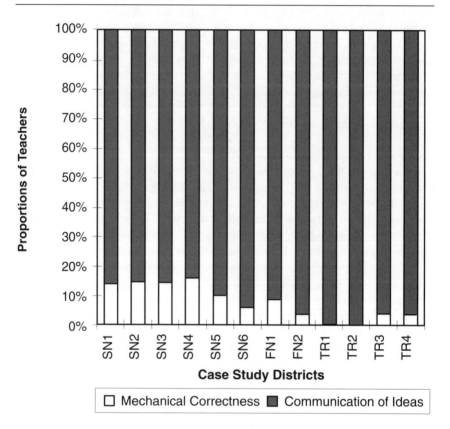

districts value communication of ideas over mechanical correctness in assessing student work in English and language arts, but the special needs districts lag slightly behind the others in this regard.

The nature of assessments may also reflect differences among districts and types of districts in the adoption of more constructivist approaches to teaching. We inquired about the use of different kinds of assessments in both the case study interviews and the teacher surveys.

Three special needs districts used some type of standardized testing, apart from state testing. One district (SN3) has aligned its curriculum very closely with these standardized tests, which are given quarterly; another (SN5) gives uniform midterms and finals in grades 4 through 12; and the third (SN2) has writing samples in grades 4, 8, and 9, and standardized departmental testing in the 4 years at the high school.

In the non–special needs districts, district-level standardized testing is fairly minimal. Three districts, however, used techniques that could fall into this category: one (FN2) formally practices for the Early Warning Test with all students in the seventh grade; another district's middle school (TR2) pretests all students in spelling; and the third (TR3) uses a writing portfolio, beginning at an early age, to assign students according to ability.

The two special needs districts most active in the move to alternative assessment as reflected in the interviews also have the most formal district-wide testing programs. These districts have begun to add many more open-ended questions to their district-wide tests so that they are more challenging and better resemble the state tests. Only one of the non–special needs districts has seriously pursued alternative assessment at the district level. This district (TR2) has eliminated standardized testing entirely for all students in grades one and two and begun to use portfolios exclusively.

At the classroom level, only TR1 has experimented with alternative assessment in any extensive way. This district sent several elementary teachers in one school to another district to observe portfolios on site. These teachers then began experimenting with portfolios in their own classrooms.

Approaches to assessment were examined on the 1994 teacher survey. Questions on that survey asked teachers to report how often they used certain kinds of techniques to assess student progress. Two items from the survey illustrate the different degrees to which English teachers have moved from traditional toward alternative assessments. One item asked teachers to report how often they used multiple-choice tests to assess student progress in English/language arts. There were significant differences among the three types of districts ($F = 21.81; p < .001$). Teachers in the special needs districts employed such traditional assessments most frequently (2.99), followed by teachers in the foundation aid districts (2.69), and those in the transition aid districts (2.40).

Figure 5.3 shows the mean responses in each of our case study districts. The three special needs districts with the most standardized testing (SN3, SN5, SN2) are also those in which the teachers report the most frequent use of multiple-choice tests. There is, however, substantial variation among the special needs districts with teachers in SN4 reporting the second-lowest frequency of use of any of the 12 districts. Foundation aid and transition aid districts also vary considerably. Teachers in TR1 reported the least frequent use of multiple-choice tests in English/language arts classes.

Another item on the teacher survey asked teachers to report on the frequency with which they used portfolios for assessment of student performance in English/language arts classes. There were no significant differences by district type, but teachers in the transition aid districts reported the most fre-

FIGURE 5.3. *Mean teacher response regarding the frequency of multiple-choice testing and portfolio use for assessing student performance in language arts*

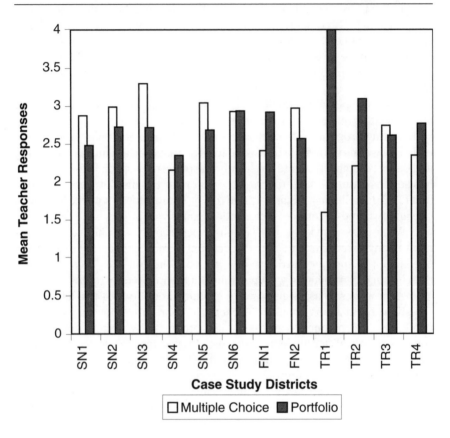

quent use (2.89), followed by teachers in foundation aid districts (2.73) and those in special needs districts (2.64).

Figure 5.3 also presents the mean responses to the question regarding the use of portfolios for the 12 case study districts. The districts range from the least frequent use of portfolios by the teachers in SN4 to the most frequent use of portfolios by the teachers in TR1. Teachers in several of the special needs districts (SN6, SN2, SN5) report more frequent use of portfolios than those in at least one transition aid district (TR3).

ENGLISH/LANGUAGE ARTS SUMMARY
Although most case study districts have adopted some curriculum, instruction, and assessment practices in English/language arts consistent with the

contemporary reform movement, our interview and teacher survey data indicate that the special needs districts continue to retain more practices consistent with their function as basic skills districts as identified by the *Abbott* court. Of course, maintaining an emphasis on skills, while adding higher order tasks, is in line with the recommendations of Delpit (1995) for teaching minority youngsters and with the conclusions of Natriello et al. (1990) for the education of at-risk students. Nevertheless, non–special needs districts are generally further along on most dimensions of practice suggested by the recent wave of reform recommendations for curriculum, instruction, and assessment in English/language arts.

The reasons why the foundation aid and transition aid districts are further along in adopting the recommendations of the current reformers in English/language arts are not difficult to understand. The special needs districts only acquired some of the resources necessary to adopt reforms like the whole language approach to reading with the passage of QEA. Some of the other districts have had such resources previously. A third grade teacher in TR2 described these resources as "phenomenal" and improving. His principal explained that the district had been preparing teachers for the whole language approach for several years through specialized training at off-site workshops during the year and in the summers. This principal also noted that a district like TR2 was well equipped to move to whole language without a great deal of expense for materials because they had a good library and many trade books available in classrooms. Ironically, moving to whole language and dropping the purchase of basal readers may end up costing this district less, not more. Districts such as TR2 were toward the end of training their entire teaching staffs in whole language during the same years that the special needs districts were just beginning to rotate teachers to such training. This difference illustrates why the special needs districts appear to lag behind the other districts in adopting the curriculum reforms.

Mathematics

Mathematics has been the subject of a focused and national movement for curriculum reform led by the reports of the National Council of Teachers of Mathematics (NCTM, 1989). The national effort to rethink curriculum, instruction, and assessment in mathematics was among the earliest in the most recent wave of subject matter reform efforts.

Mathematics Curriculum

Among the recommendations for changing math curricula have been calls for both a more constructivist approach to mathematics and calls for greater attention to application. Constructivism and application have taken root, in some form or another, in almost all 12 of our districts. The one district (TR3) that has not moved in this direction has had a very competitive and success-ful program thus far; they did not want to make seemingly unnecessary changes. With this one exception, curriculum coordinators at the district level uniformly claimed that they no longer were teaching computation skills in isolation, and that math meant problem solving and understanding, not just arithmetic.

The math coordinator in SN2 described the district's embrace of the NCTM reforms:

> The NCTM standards have been our guiding light. We encourage new cre-ative strategies on the part of teachers. We don't want conventional math teachers. We sent teachers to workshops, and we used resources within the district. . . . We do a lot in our department meetings . . . a lot of in-district dialogue and communication. . . . We introduced pre-calculus with 2 classes this year. Next year we will have 19 kids in calculus. . . . We are moving beyond basic math.

This coordinator gave a specific example of a practice designed to make sure students were moved beyond basic computation:

> If a kid can't do basic computation by the sixth grade we give him a calcu-lator . . . we don't want this to stand in the way of their thinking. . . . Computation is not math, that's arithmetic.

Moreover, the coordinator extended the new approach to math into the basic-skills program and now supervises the basic-skills teachers as well as the regular math teachers. He explained how he has integrated the approach in basic-skills classes with the district's overall approach to math:

> We now have the basic-skills teachers meet with the math teachers. There is a lot more coordination between basic-skills and regular teachers. So now basic skills is manipulatives and problem-solving.

As with language arts, the 1994 teacher survey included an item related to the approach to mathematics taken in the districts that allowed us to check the information provided in the interviews. Teachers were asked to indi-cate what mathematics represented in their school and were given three choices representing different conceptions of the field:

> Mathematics is primarily a system of established procedures and rules that always produce the same result.
> Mathematics is primarily a language that facilitates the generation of creative approaches to problem solving.
> Mathematics is primarily a tool for everyday life.

The first conception of mathematics as a set of rules and procedures is a traditional view of the field. The second conception emphasizing the generation of creative approaches to solving problems is more constructivist. The third conception focusing on math as a tool embodies a more applied approach. The patterns of teacher responses reflect the overall movement of districts toward the new math standards.

Teachers in all three types of districts avoided the rules and procedures option. Only 8.4% of teachers in special needs districts, 11.1% of teachers in foundation aid districts, and 7.1% of those in transition aid districts selected this traditional conception of mathematics. Although teachers in all three types of districts were more likely to select either the constructivist or applied conception of math, teachers in the special needs districts were more likely to identify the applied conception of mathematics as characterizing the approach in their district (53.2%) than teachers in either the foundation aid districts (42.2%) or those in the transition aid districts (43.9%). The constructivist conception of mathematics as a language to facilitate creative problem solving was selected by 49% of teachers in transition aid districts, 46.7% of teachers in foundation aid districts, and 38.4% of those in special needs districts.

Figure 5.4 portrays the distributions of teacher responses across the three conceptions of mathematics for each of the 12 case study districts. The rule-based conception of mathematics was indicated by as many as 17.5% of the teachers in SN6 to as few as 0% of the teachers in TR2 and TR1. The constructivist conception of mathematics was selected by over half of the teachers in three of the four transition aid districts (TR4, TR2, and TR1), in one of the two foundation aid districts (FN1), and in none of the special needs districts. The applied conception of mathematics was chosen by over half of the teachers in five of the six special needs districts (SN1, SN2, SN3, SN4, and SN5).

In sum, teachers in the special needs districts, like those in non–special needs districts, are moving beyond the traditional approach to teaching math; they are, however, more likely to select an applied rather than a constructivist alternative.

A few comments about the organization of the mathematics curriculum in the 12 districts are necessary. Mathematics is tracked in all the high schools in our study, regardless of district type; the number of tracks ranges from three to five. The special needs districts, however, have more sections of low or remedial tracks, while the non–special needs districts have more sections of high-level math.

Districts also differ in the extent of district-to-school consistency within math curricula. While three special needs districts (SN2, SN3, SN4) had considerable alignment between the central office and the schools, the others lacked this consistency. In two cases, the schools varied widely in their

FIGURE 5.4. *Proportions of teachers indicating the primary conception of mathematics in their school*

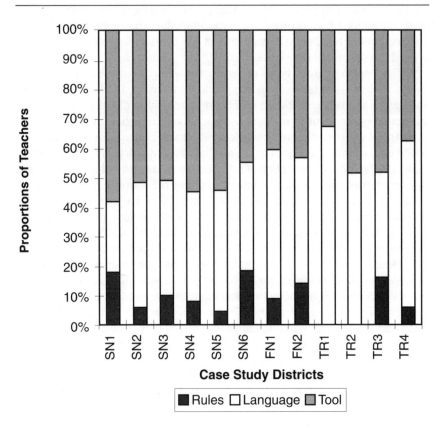

approaches to the curriculum (SN5, SN6); in the third (SN1), the director in the central office was far ahead compared to what was happening in the schools.

Again, in the non–special needs districts, there is little central office influence, because most of these small districts have small central office staffs. Often the schools drive the curriculum (TR2, TR3, TR4). In the few larger districts, curricula also tend to be consistent (FN2, TR1); only one district's curricular approaches (FN1), which were consistent from kindergarten through eighth grade, did not match well with those stated in the high school.

INSTRUCTION IN MATHEMATICS

Several instructional techniques have been designated as compatible with the latest thinking in mathematics education. These include the use of manipulatives to facilitate learning, the use of calculators to relieve the stress on computation, the incorporation of computers into math instruction, increased attention to writing in math instruction through devices such as writing journals, and cooperative learning as a basis for group problem solving. We examined elements of these instructional techniques in both our site visits and the teacher surveys.

The case study interviews in the special needs districts revealed a range of intensity with which manipulatives have become integrated into the curriculum. Four districts use them with some consistency: two (SN3, SN4) have a high emphasis in kindergarten through eighth grade; one (SN2) has a high emphasis at one elementary school; and one (SN5) has introduced them in the high school. The two other special needs districts (SN1, SN6) have not begun to do much with manipulatives thus far. The results of the teacher surveys presented in Table 5.5 reveal similar, but not identical, patterns. The two districts that appeared not to be using manipulatives in the site visits (SN1, SN6), are among the lowest in reported use by teachers, but teachers in SN4, which was reported using manipulatives in grades K through 8 by the site visit team, also reported less-frequent use.

Three non–special needs districts (FN1, TR1, TR2) have relatively high emphasis on manipulatives. These districts have integrated manipulatives into their math programs. Respondents in two of the districts (TR3, TR4) mention the high level of access for their students, but suggest only a moderate amount of attention given to instruction with manipulatives. Finally, one district (FN2) has simply low emphasis on manipulative use. The results of the teacher surveys generally confirm these patterns as indicated in Table 5.5. The use of manipulatives is highest in the transition aid districts and lowest in the special needs districts with the foundation aid districts falling in between. These differences by district type are significant ($F = 4.52, p < .05$).

Calculator use is equally varied as manipulative use in the special needs districts. In the interviews two districts (SN2, SN4) show high emphasis, one across the entire district and one at the high school and one elementary school. Respondents in one district (SN3) suggest access to calculators but not much classroom emphasis. And in the other three (SN1, SN5, SN6), those interviewed suggest that high emphasis is impossible because of a lack of calculators.

These patterns apparent in the case study reports are also reflected in the teacher surveys. As indicated in the fourth column of Table 5.5, the three districts where those interviewed reported limited access to calculators (SN1, SN5, SN6) are those in which teachers report the least-frequent use.

The case study reports also suggest that of the non–special needs districts, the two middle-income districts (FN1, FN2) have problems with incomplete access. However, the other four districts all have very complete access, although three (TR1, TR2, TR3) only modestly emphasize calculator use.

Only one district (TR4) claims that in addition to offering full access, calculators have revolutionized math instruction.

The results of the teacher surveys presented in Table 5-5 confirm the full access reported by representatives in TR4; teachers in this district report the most frequent use of calculators, with the exception of the limited sample of four teachers in TR1 who report even more frequent access. As with manipulatives, the greatest use of calculators is in the transition aid districts, and the least is in the special needs districts. These differences by district type are significant ($F = 7.34, p < .001$).

TABLE 5.5. *Mean teacher responses regarding the frequency of use of manipulatives, calculators, and computers in mathematics classes, by district*

DISTRICT	MANIPULATIVES		CALCULATORS		COMPUTERS	
	MEAN	N	MEANS	N	MEANS	N
SN1	2.24	66	2.12	52	1.90	52
SN2	2.99	88	2.71	76	2.32	77
SN3	3.04	114	2.66	111	2.18	87
SN4	2.77	71	2.43	72	2.35	65
SN5	3.02	175	2.39	142	2.05	116
SN6	2.90	40	2.24	34	2.22	36
FN1	3.12	33	2.56	27	2.14	29
FN2	2.95	59	2.64	50	2.40	52
TR1	3.33	6	4.00	4	1.00	6
TR2	3.30	37	2.90	29	2.48	31
TR3	3.04	54	2.36	47	2.65	52
TR4	3.05	57	3.12	58	2.38	53
SN	2.89[a]	554	2.47[b]	487	2.17[c]	433
FN	3.01	92	2.61	77	2.31	81
TR	3.12	154	2.84	138	2.44	142
All districts	2.95	800	2.56	702	2.25	656

Responses: 1 = never or hardly ever, 2 = once or twice a month, 3 = once or twice a week, 4 = almost every day.
[a] $F = 4.52, p < .05$
[b] $F = 7.34, p < .001$
[c] $F = 3.86, p < .05$

The teacher surveys also offer information on the use of computers in mathematics instruction. The sixth column of Table 5.5 presents the mean teacher responses for the frequency of computer use by students for mathematics instruction. Responses ranged from about 2 (indicating once or twice a month) in SN1 (1.9) and SN5 (2.1) to somewhat more than this in SN4 (2.4) and SN2 (2.3). Among the non–special needs districts the responses ranged from 2.1 in FN1 to 2.7 in TR3 with the six respondents in TR1 all reporting that computers were never or hardly ever used in math instruction. The use of computers is significantly more frequent in the transition aid districts and least common in the special needs districts ($F = 3.86$, $p < .05$).

Math journals are another practice associated with the new approach to mathematics instruction. From the site visits we learned that there is relatively little use of math journals in any of our 12 districts. Only one special needs district has adopted the technique and is currently using it in kindergarten through eighth grade. Three non–special needs districts use journals, although in these districts the practice is either occurring in the middle schools (FN1, TR1) or the high school (TR4).

No item on the teacher survey corresponded directly to math journals, but teachers were asked how often they required students to write a few sentences about how to solve a mathematics problem. Table 5.6, second column, reports on the responses to this question. Among the special needs districts the responses ranged from less than once or twice a month in SN1 (1.8), SN6 (1.8), and SN4 (1.97) to closer to once or twice a week in SN5 (2.6). A similar range was found among the non–special needs districts, with a low of 1.9 in TR3 to a high of 2.7 in TR1.

Although we inquired about cooperative learning in our site visits, there appeared to be no pattern across district types. Two special needs districts (SN2, SN5) adopted the practice at the elementary level, while one (SN3) is using it at the middle school. One non–special needs district (TR4) has adopted the practice at the elementary level, and one (TR1) is using it at the high school.

An item on the teacher survey asked teachers to report how often math students worked in small groups. This is not the same as cooperative learning, which may explain the different patterns of findings. The fourth column of Table 5.6 presents the teacher responses to this item. Among the special needs districts group work seemed relatively common, occurring more than once or twice a week in three of the six districts (SN3, 3.22; SN5, 3.18; SN2, 3.10). In the other special needs districts teachers reported using small groups for instruction in math close to once or twice a week. The same kind of pattern appeared in the responses of teachers in the non–special needs districts. Mean responses ranged from 2.86 in FN2 to 3.22 in TR4.

Overall, the patterns for mathematics instruction in the 12 case study districts reveal that in three of the five instructional practices examined, the

TABLE 5.6. *Means teacher responses regarding the frequency of assignments involving writing sentences and frequency of group work in mathematics class, by district*

| | WRITING SENTENCES | | GROUP WORK | |
DISTRICT	MEAN	N	MEAN	N
SN1	1.84	58	2.63	64
SN2	2.00	78	3.10	90
SN3	2.28	107	3.22	115
SN4	1.97	62	2.66	68
SN5	2.56	148	3.18	174
SN6	1.84	33	2.73	41
FN1	2.42	24	2.86	36
FN2	2.06	49	3.04	55
TR1	2.67	6	3.00	6
TR2	2.56	27	3.14	35
TR3	1.86	43	2.88	49
TR4	2.30	54	3.22	59
SN	2.20[a]	486	3.21[b]	552
FN	2.18	53	2.97	91
TR	2.22	130	3.08	149
All districts	2.20	689	3.02	792

Responses: 1 = never or hardly ever, 2 = once or twice a month, 3 = once or twice a week, 4 = almost every day.
[a] $F = .053$, NS
[b] $F = 620$, NS

special needs districts lagged and the transition aid districts led in adoption. Certain special needs districts appear to be behind in the implementation of these instructional approaches suggested by recent reform recommendations. Teachers in SN1 report the lowest incidence of the use of manipulatives, calculators, computers, writing about mathematics, and cooperative learning. Teachers in SN4 report relatively less frequent use of manipulatives, writing in mathematics, and cooperative learning. SN6 is among the districts least likely to be using manipulatives, calculators, writing in mathematics, and cooperative learning. Thus three of the special needs districts, SN1, SN4, and SN6, appear to be especially behind in the movement toward new instructional approaches in mathematics.

ASSESSMENT IN MATHEMATICS

Reform recommendations have also been made regarding the assessment of student performance in mathematics. Examining the patterns of assessment employed in mathematics in the 12 districts provides additional support for our view that while personnel in all of the districts are aware of and influenced by the reform recommendations, some special needs districts are implementing new practices at a slower pace than the non–special needs districts.

A question from the 1994 teacher survey asked teachers to choose between the "correct answer" and a "reasonable explanation" as the most important criterion for evaluating student performance in mathematics; the former is most consistent with traditional approaches to the teaching of mathematics, the latter is most consistent with the approaches recommended as part of the new mathematics reforms. Figure 5.5 shows the responses of the teachers in the 12 districts to this item.

The proportions of teachers citing the correct answer as the most important criterion for evaluating student work in mathematics range from 0% in TR1 to 40.3% in SN1. Thirty percent or more of the teachers cited the correct answer as the most important criterion in four of the six special needs districts, while the highest proportion of teachers citing it among the non–special needs districts was 25.9% in FN2. Although only a minority of teachers in all of the 12 districts indicated that the correct answer was the most important criterion in evaluating student work in mathematics, there are differences among districts with fewer teachers in the transition aid districts and more teachers in the special needs districts indicating it was the most important criterion. These differences among types of districts did not reach statistical significance.

Another indicator of the patterns of assessment practices employed by school districts is the use of standardized tests. There is a considerable difference in the use of district-wide standardized testing (not state mandated) in the area of mathematics across district types. Four of the six special needs districts use some form of this assessment: two (SN3, SN5) have extensive testing for almost all grade levels, while two (SN2, SN1) have tests at each marking period in the high schools. In contrast, none of the non–special needs districts uses district-wide standardized testing in math.

The pattern of teacher use of multiple-choice tests in mathematics, as reported in Figure 5.6, is quite different from the pattern for district-wide standardized tests. Indeed, the top two districts in teacher-reported use of multiple-choice tests in mathematics are transition aid districts (TR3, TR2). Only one special needs district (SN5) is among the top five districts in teacher use of multiple-choice tests. This pattern reflects the continued use of traditional assessment practices among non–special needs districts and is consistent with the image of non–special needs districts as adding constructivist elements to

FIGURE 5.5. *Proportions of teachers indicating correct answer and reasonable explanation as the most important criterion for evaluating student performance in mathematics*

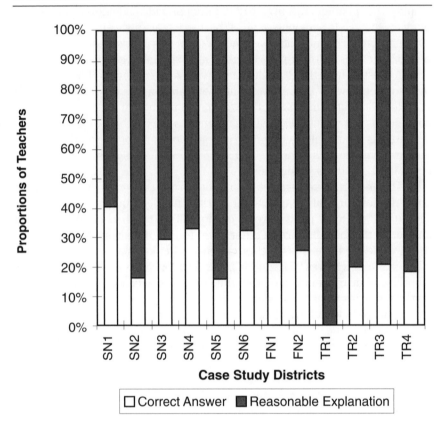

their traditional approaches rather than replacing traditional approaches with constructivist ones.

The use of alternative assessment techniques is another indicator of district approaches to assessment in mathematics. Our findings from the site visits show little use of alternative assessment at the district or classroom levels in math. Two special needs districts made small attempts; for example, one (SN3) adjusted questions on its district-wide test so that they resemble the new, more-challenging format of questions on the state test, and one (SN2) worked with a community college on portfolio assessment. But none of the special needs districts seemed to have any activity at the classroom level in terms of alternative assessment.

FIGURE 5.6. *Mean teacher responses regarding the frequency of multiple-choice testing and portfolio use for assessing student performance in mathematics*

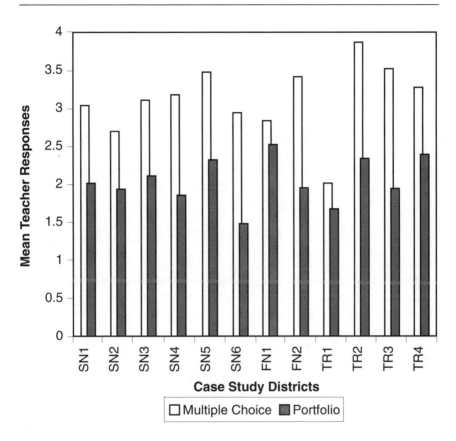

Likewise in the non–special needs districts, only one district (TR2) changed district-level assessment; this is the same district that eliminated standardized testing for all students in grades one and two, and now uses portfolios exclusively in these grades. However, at the classroom level three districts noted some activity. In two of these districts (FN1, TR1), teachers have been experimenting with portfolios individually. And in the other district (TR4), teachers have been actively trying to include many more open-ended questions in their assessments.

This pattern of relatively low use of alternative assessment techniques is confirmed in the teacher surveys. Figure 5.6 also shows the mean responses of teachers in the 12 districts to a question about the frequency with which they used portfolios to assess student progress in mathematics. Responses included 1 ("Never or hardly ever"), 2 ("Once or twice a year"), 3 ("Once or twice a month"), 4 ("Once or twice a week"). Teachers in all 12 districts reported relatively infrequent use of portfolios; teachers in five of the 12 districts reported an average frequency for the use of portfolios of less than once or twice a year.

MATH SUMMARY

All case study districts are moving beyond traditional approaches to curriculum, but there is some tendency for special needs districts to move toward an applied approach while non–special needs districts move toward a constructivist approach. In terms of specific instructional approaches, the special needs districts are lagging behind the other districts in adoption. As for assessment, all of the case study districts report some movement beyond traditional approaches to assessment, but the movement is rather slight.

CONCLUSIONS

We began this chapter by considering the state and national climate for the renewal and reform of curriculum, instruction, and assessment in English/language arts and mathematics. We set about investigating how these reform efforts might affect different types of districts subject to different effects from the QEA.

The prevailing opinion that the special needs districts in 1990 in New Jersey lagged behind in the adoption and implementation of new curriculum and instructional approaches was confirmed in our initial case study site visits. The special needs districts were behind the non–special needs districts in the movement to incorporate higher order thinking skills in the curriculum and in the adoption of strategies such as whole language instruction in English/language arts, and the practices suggested by the NCTM standards in mathematics.

Our initial interviews revealed that special needs districts had resource deficits that prevented them from adopting new curricular approaches or at least slowed them down substantially. District staff explained that prior to QEA they might be able to acquire a new text series to organize an area of the curriculum, but that they seldom had the resources to purchase the related materials. Moreover, when they did adopt a new curriculum, they seldom had the staff development resources to prepare all teachers to implement the new system. Thus, as they entered the 1990s, the special needs districts trailed other districts in terms of curriculum renewal.

Although the special needs districts were not as responsive to the national curriculum reform movements as the non–special needs districts in the period prior to the QEA, they appeared to be as responsive or more responsive to state assessment activities. The special needs districts were more likely to be affected by the state testing program than other districts because their students were more likely to experience difficulty with the test. As a result, staff in the special needs districts were quite aware of the state testing program and had adapted their instructional programs to prepare students for the High School Proficiency Test. Moreover, staff in the special needs districts were as likely or more likely than staff in other districts to have adjusted their programs in anticipation of the new 11th grade High School Proficiency Test.

With the advent of the QEA in 1991, the additional monies made available to the special needs districts enabled them to engage in the kind of curriculum development and renewal that other districts had always undertaken. Those special needs district staff interviewed as part of our site visits explained that for the first time in memory, their districts could purchase new texts in a subject for all grade levels so that the overall program could be coordinated. Moreover, special needs districts were able to acquire the related materials that teachers needed to implement fully the new curricula. Finally, staff in special needs districts reported receiving staff development to support the new curricular efforts, something that had not been as available previously. The QEA did not drive program renewal in the special needs districts; rather, for the first time, the funds from the QEA enabled the special needs districts to participate in the national movement in subject matter renewal in which other districts had typically been active prior to the QEA.

The special needs districts did use the additional funds from the QEA to renew their curricula. As the data in this chapter reveal, the districts differed in the degree to which they were able to move in the directions suggested by the reformers. Districts like SN2 and SN3 moved further than others such as SN1 and SN6.

As for the non–special needs districts, while generally further along in adopting the reform agenda than the special needs districts, they, too, differed in the degree to which they embraced the current reforms, with some leading and others lagging in this movement. The variation within groups of districts with historically disparate levels of available resources suggests that at least some of the differences in the pace of reform are attributable to such nonfiscal factors as the educational philosophies that dominate districts and communities.

Although the special needs districts engaged in curriculum renewal in the wake of the QEA, the question remains as to their current position in relation to the non–special needs districts. The site visit interviews and the teacher surveys suggest that the non–special needs districts are still ahead of those in poor urban areas in implementing the current reform agenda. The advantages for the non–special needs districts are stronger in the case of language arts, where reform activities among professional groups have been ongoing and where most educators are confident of their skills. The inequity inherent in the offerings of these different types of districts may only be mitigated over a longer period of time with continuing commitments of resources to the renewal and development of the instructional programs in the historically disadvantaged special needs districts. And of course, special needs districts may be more likely to retain their traditional skills-based approaches as well, to meet the needs of their student populations. Overall, the developments in curriculum, instruction, and assessment even in the wake of a substantially reduced QEA seem to suggest at least the beginning of the kind of experimentation and development mentioned in the *Abbott* decision.

6

SERVICES FOR AT-RISK STUDENTS

I n Chapters 4 and 5 we examined the impact of the Quality Education Act (QEA) on staffing, curriculum, instruction, and assessment in the general education program. As we saw in Chapter 3, however, the special needs districts in our sample used some of the additional resources available through the QEA to address the growing social problems facing their students. In this chapter we discuss these social problems, the programmatic responses mounted by the districts, and the challenges that remain. The social conditions from which students come pose special risks for the students and impose special burdens on local districts. For the special needs districts these burdens were quite substantial.

At-risk students is the identifying term applied to those students who have a greater than average chance of not succeeding in school and graduating. Frost (1994) reports that the majority of states have incorporated the term *at-risk* as a label for students in education legislation. As Frost notes, most of the definitions used in legislation involve environmental factors in combination with individual characteristics. This legislation is usually directed at providing special programs or resources for the targeted group of students to improve their educational outcomes. New Jersey is no exception to this pattern.

The early identification of students as being at-risk might lead to their assignment to appropriate programs designed to help them achieve school success or it might lead to pejorative labeling and the self-fulfilling prophecy that consigns such students to exposure to lower teacher expectations for their entire school careers. Thus it is particularly important to understand the extent and nature of programs intended to address the special needs of students at-risk.

DISADVANTAGED STUDENTS AND SCHOOLING

There are multiple ways of thinking about students as being disadvantaged when it comes to their chances of succeeding in school. Some scholars have focused on cultural or social deprivation of these students such as inadequate family situations, personal deficiencies such as auditory or visual limitations, or social group characteristics such as low socioeconomic status and minority racial or ethnic group status (Bernstein, 1960; Gordon & Yowell, 1994; Havighurst, 1965; Passow & Elliott, 1967). Others have considered educational deprivation based in social, political, or cultural factors that have limited or restricted access to the educational system (Passow, 1970). Still others have conceived of a combination of individual and environmental characteristics that limit students' access to paths to success and increase their susceptibility to certain barriers to success in schooling (Montgomery & Rossi, 1994). This perspective, which links individual and environmental factors, is represented in Levin's (1986) point that "pupils defined as educationally disadvantaged lack the home and community resources to fully benefit from recent educational reforms as well as from conventional schooling practices" (p. 1).

These perspectives lead to a definition of *educationally disadvantaged* that considers students' experiences in the home, the community, and the school. Natriello et al. (1990) suggest that students are educationally disadvantaged if they have been exposed to insufficient educational experiences in at least one of these three domains. They go on to identify a number of indicators that signal such problems in each area.

Minority racial or ethnic status has been associated with educational disadvantage. Hispanic and black students perform less well in school than nonminority students, though in recent years the gap in achievement has been narrowing (National Center for Education Statistics, 1994a). Poverty has also been connected with poor educational performance and lower attainment. For example, children living in families with incomes below the poverty line are nearly twice as likely to be retained in grade as those from non-poverty-stricken families (Bianchi, 1984). Certain family configurations, particularly single-parent families, are also thought to contribute to educational disadvantage. Children living in homes with single parents score lower on standardized assessments of performance (Natriello et al., 1990). Among whites and Hispanics, these children are more likely to drop out of school (Ekstrom, Goertz, Pollack, & Rock 1987). The educational level of mothers is yet another indicator of educational disadvantage. Children whose mothers have not completed high school score lower on the National Assessment of Educational Progress (NAEP) than those whose mothers have completed high school (Natriello et al., 1990), and maternal education is also related to the likelihood of dropping out of school (Barro & Kolstad, 1987). Finally, limited English proficiency is also an indicator of some educational disadvantage. Students who are exposed to or speak a language other than English at home score lower on both the NAEP reading test and the NAEP math test (Natriello et al., 1990). Moreover, there is at least some evidence that such students are more likely to drop out of school (Salganik & Celebuski, 1987). In Chapter 3 we saw that students in the special needs districts are substantially more likely to experience each of these disadvantaging conditions than students in the other districts in our case study sample.

While social scientists study these background indicators, state policy makers often focus on more proximate indicators of special educational needs. In recent years policies in a number of states have concentrated on students with lower achievement levels and those at risk of dropping out of school (Coley & Goertz, 1990). These indicators often trigger a response from state policy makers.

In New Jersey, as in many other states, two specific indicators used to identify students with special needs have been scores on the state-mandated competency tests and graduation rates. Before reviewing the programs available for at-risk students in the 12 case study districts, we examine these indicators. The High School Proficiency Test (HSPT) contains sections on reading, mathematics, and writing. Figure 6.1 reports on the proportions of eleventh grade students passing each section of the test and the proportions passing all three sections of the test in October 1993 (New Jersey State Department of Education, 1994). Substantially fewer students pass these tests in the special needs districts. Among special needs districts the range of proportions passing the reading section extends from 43.8% in SN1 to 77.9% in SN4, with an average rate of 60.9%. In the foundation aid districts the average proportion passing the reading test is 90.1%, in the transition aid districts, 93.4%.

The same pattern holds for the math test. There the range of proportions passing among students in the special needs districts extends from 27.9% in SN1 to 76.1% in SN4, with an average rate of 55.4%. In the foundation aid districts the average proportion passing the math test is 89.0%, and in the transition aid districts, 94.1%.

The differences among districts and district types are less dramatic for the writing test. Among special needs districts the range of passing rates extends from 75.7% in SN6 to 89.4% in SN4, with an average rate of 81.5% passing. In the foundation aid districts the average proportion passing the writing test is 96.2%, and in the transition aid districts, 97.0%.

The proportions passing all three sections of the HSPT mirror the results for the individual sections. Among special needs districts the range extends from 21.2% of students in SN1 to 65.5% in SN4, with an average of 43.6% of students passing all three sections. In the foundation aid districts the average passing rate is 81.7%, and in the transition aid districts, 89.0%. These patterns

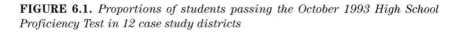

FIGURE 6.1. *Proportions of students passing the October 1993 High School Proficiency Test in 12 case study districts*

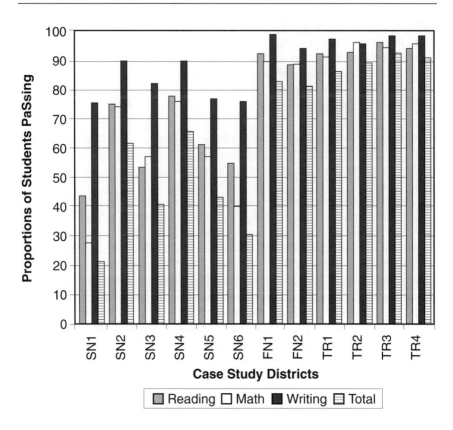

observed among the districts in our case studies are also apparent statewide. In 1993/94, only 41.5% of the students in the 30 special needs districts passed all three sections of the HSPT, compared to 80% of students in the non–special needs districts statewide. Performance on the eighth grade Early Warning Test (EWT) mirrored that of the HSPT. The overall pattern is quite clear and consistent; the special needs districts serve large numbers of students who have difficulty mastering the skills contained in the state testing program.

Not surprisingly, these districts also have large numbers of students who do not complete their high school education. Figure 6.2 presents the high school graduation rates for students in the 12 case study districts in 1990 (Bureau of Government Research and Department of Government Services. 1992). These rather unrefined estimates, calculated by dividing the number of high school

FIGURE 6.2. *Proportions of students graduating from high school in the 12 case study districts in 1990*

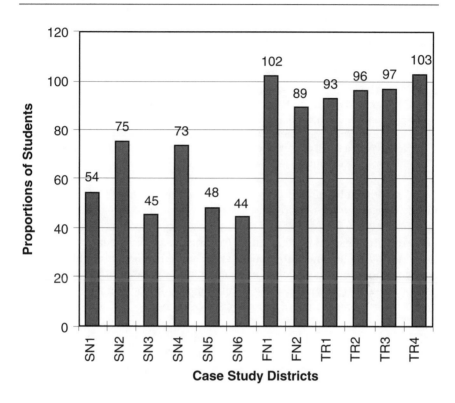

graduates in 1990 by the enrollment in the ninth grade in 1986, result in some anomalies (such as graduation rates exceeding 100%) caused by students moving into the district after the ninth grade. Nonetheless, they provide a serviceable indicator of graduation and dropout rates for comparing students in the different types of districts. As Figure 6.2 indicates, among the special needs districts the graduation rates range from 44% in SN6 to 75% in SN2, for an average rate among the special needs districts of 57%. In the foundation aid districts the average graduation rate was 96%, and in the transition aid districts, 97%. Thus, while over 40% of the students in the special needs districts did not graduate from high school, fewer than 5% of the students in the non–special needs districts failed to graduate. On a wide range of background and performance indicators, the students served by the special needs districts are clearly at greater risk of failing in school than the students in the non–special needs districts. Such students present particular challenges for the special needs districts. These students impose burdens that simply do not apply to other districts.

The New Jersey Supreme Court recognized that students in poor urban communities like those in the special needs districts in our study have extensive social and economic needs that can hinder their performance in school. The court wrote that:

> These needs go beyond educational needs, they include food, clothing and shelter, and extend to lack of close family and community ties and support, and lack of helpful role models. They include the needs that arise from a life led in an environment of violence, poverty and despair. . . . Education forms only a small part of their home life, sometimes no part of their school life, and the dropout is almost the norm. (*Abbott II* at 369)

The court identified programs that have the potential to address these disadvantages—intensive preschool and all-day kindergarten enrichment programs to reverse the educational disadvantage poor students bring to school; adequate libraries and media centers to compensate for the lack of books at home; adequate guidance programs to give children individual attention; counseling services to help students overcome problems associated with teenage pregnancies, drugs, and unstable family environments; and alternative programs for students at risk of dropping out of school.

The justices then noted that many of these programs are provided in richer suburban districts. The poorer urban districts, however, could not afford them. As a result, the court ordered the state to "provide for the special educational needs of these poorer urban districts and address their extreme disadvantages" (*Abbott II* at 385).

STATE SUPPORT FOR PROGRAMS FOR AT-RISK STUDENTS

In response to the court's mandate, the legislature created a program of *aid for students at risk of educational failure* under the QEA. As shown in Table 2.1, the state allocated $293 million in at-risk aid in 1993/94, a $143 million increase over the compensatory education aid program it replaced. The 30 special needs districts received $183 million of this aid, a $104 million increase over 1990/91. The state allocated the at-risk aid based on a student poverty measure, providing between $1,092 (grades pre-K to 5) and $1,461 (grades 9 to 12) for each public school student who was eligible for the federal free lunch or free milk programs. But, the funds could be spent on any student deemed at-risk. State regulations defined "at-risk" students broadly, as those "who are at risk of not acquiring the knowledge, skills, behaviors and attitudes necessary for school success, school completion, and successful functioning as an adult in society" (*New Jersey Register*, 1992). Unlike the old compensatory education aid program, which was targeted on remedial education programs, at-risk aid could be used for prevention, intervention, or programs that improve the learning environment. However, the programs and services provided by districts had to include assistance for students performing below state-established performance standards.

The QEA also supported the costs of *early childhood programs* operated by public school districts. Under the foundation aid formula, districts eligible for foundation aid received funds for students who were enrolled in pre-kindergarten (4 year olds) and full-day kindergarten classes in their schools. Aid was allocated, however, using a count of students served in the previous year. Thus, districts had to use their own resources to establish or expand early childhood programs in the first year of operation. Finding these funds was difficult in the poor communities because of their limited tax bases and competing demands for both educational and noneducational services.

To address these problems, the New Jersey Department of Education (SDE) established a program designed to provide start-up money for urban preschool programs. Called GoodStarts, the program allocated $6 million in state lottery funds and a $2 million federal grant to provide preschool education for children in the special needs districts. Begun in 1992, the program provides preschool to children turned away from Head Start. In 1995 the program paid for nearly 41,000 children to attend preschool and receive extra services through the second grade.

State education aid does not provide earmarked funding for student health services (Anderson, 1995). While the typical school nurse plays an important role, this level of health services was never designed to address the kinds of problems that students bring to the school door today, especially in poor communities. These problems include substance abuse, unplanned and unwanted pregnancy, mental and physical abuse, suicide and homicide of family members, depression and alienation, and limited access to regular medical services. In an attempt to address the major physical and mental health needs of New Jersey's youth, the state department of human services, in collaboration with departments of labor, education, and health, established a pilot *School Based Youth Services Program* (SBYS) in 1988. The program, which received $7 million of funding in 1993, provides comprehensive services in or near 37 elementary, middle, and high schools across the state, including schools in three of the six special needs districts in our study. Sites are managed by nonprofit and community agencies, local governments, and schools. Each site, which receives about $200,000 from the state and contributes a 25% local match in dollars or in-kind services, provides a core set of services: mental health and family counseling, primary and preventive health care, employment services, substance abuse services, recreation, and referral to social and medical services, with follow-up. The programs may choose to provide additional services, such as family planning, teen parenting education, and academic tutoring.

Although the state introduced several new programs to respond to the needs of poor children in the early 1990s, these programs did not begin to address the full extent of the problems posed by poverty conditions for the state's children. The primary responsibility for ameliorating the effects of poverty on the educational process remained with the local districts. Indeed, the special needs districts were able to become more involved in responding to the social problems of students following the passage of the QEA.

PROGRAMMATIC RESPONSES TO AT-RISK STUDENTS AT THE DISTRICT LEVEL

As indicated above, districts had considerable leeway in how they used their at-risk aid, and in the types and scope of the programs they developed for their students. All special needs districts in our study included support services as a major component of their mission and as objectives in their Education Improvement Plans (EIPs). These objectives included the provision of early childhood and full-day kindergarten programs; breakfast and lunch programs; more social support services, such as counselors; increased student attendance monitoring; increased parental involvement in the schools; and the provision of facilities to house these expanded programs.

While all six districts aimed to provide a comparable set of social services to their students, the specific actions they took differed. The strategies and programs that districts chose reflected the interaction of four factors: (1) the needs of the students in the district, (2) the existing level of services, (3) available funds, and (4) available space. This section describes the major actions that the districts in our study took under the QEA to respond to the special needs of their students. It begins with a typology of at-risk programs that we use to frame our presentation. We then identify the major academic and social programs that the districts initiated, and consider the patterns of their responses.

A Typology of At-Risk Programs

Programs for at-risk students can be considered along a number of dimensions. In this study, we considered programs along two dimensions identified in earlier research (Montgomery et al., 1993; Natriello et al., 1990). The first considers whether the program addresses the *academic* or the *social or emotional needs of students;* the second specifies the *locus of the problems* confronting students that the programs are designed to ameliorate as either internal to the school or in the wider external environment in which students are living. Figure 6.3 depicts this typology.

Academic internal needs pertain to difficulties that students experience with the regular school program. These needs can be addressed by programs designed to help students achieve academic success in school, such as providing additional instruction for students, perhaps through tutoring or adapting existing instruction to match student skill levels more closely. *Academic external* needs are related to the perceived value of student academic performance in the wider environment beyond the school. At-risk students often perceive little connection between their present academic performance and valued rewards outside the school, either in the present or in the future. Programs that expose students to individuals in the community, especially those of their own gender or racial/ethnic background, who have succeeded as a result of academic achievement as well as programs that link students to post-secondary opportunities can make that connection clearer and more meaningful. Adult mentoring programs and school-to-work transition programs are two ways to address this problem.

Social internal needs relate to the immediate social environment of the school. At-risk students sometimes experience a lack of connection to the school as an institution and to teachers and students, particularly in larger middle and high schools. Restructuring large schools into smaller houses, or schools-within-a-school, or programs that seek to strengthen the connection of stu-

FIGURE 6.3. *A typology of programs for at-risk students*

	Internal	**External**
Academic	Academic Internal	Academic External
Examples	*Tutoring*	*Mentoring*
Social	Social Internal	Social External
Examples	*House Plan*	*Health Clinic*

dents to others, like peer counseling, attempt to reduce this sense of alienation. Social service programs, such as school-based youth services, focus primarily on *social external needs*. They are needs that arise from the social conditions in the families and the communities in which students reside that make it more difficult for them to concentrate their efforts on school work: poverty, single-parent families, families with health problems or substance abuse problems, and communities plagued by violence.

The 12 case study districts used programs in each of the four categories of the typology to respond to the needs of at-risk students. The resources available through the QEA appeared to allow these districts to move beyond their initial concentration on academic internal needs of their students to add programs and program elements that responded more to social needs and external needs. Thus, whereas earlier state policies such as the mandated testing program influenced districts to focus on academic internal needs, the QEA enabled them to adopt a broader portfolio of programs to meet a wider range of student needs.

Academic Programs for At-Risk Students

Even in the wake of QEA the largest number of programs addressed the academic internal needs of students; a smaller number addressed the connections between success in school and success in the broader environment. Often programs would contain elements that addressed both internal and external academic needs of students. More specifically, we found that the districts in this study used a mix of the following programs to address the academic needs of their students who were at-risk of failing in school: (1) compensatory education, (2) early childhood education, (3) alternative schools, and (4) after-school programs.

COMPENSATORY EDUCATION

The special needs districts used more than half of their at-risk monies to fund compensatory education programs. In New Jersey districts must provide compensatory education services to students who score below state standards on mandated assessments. Districts have additional incentives to help their students, as those who do not pass the eleventh grade High School Proficiency Test (HSPT) will not receive a diploma, and at least 75% of students in each of their schools must meet state achievement standards at all three grade levels (4th, 8th, 11th) for the district to receive state certification. The cost of remediation in the special needs districts reflects the high failure rates on the state's tests as shown in Figure 6.1.

The special needs districts in our study generally provided the same level and type of remedial services as in the past. At least one district, SN4, gave its elementary schools the option of replacing their remedial pull-out program with instructional aides in the classroom. This change, which reflected the philosophy of the director of special programs, also freed up teachers and classrooms for the district's growing primary grade population. In response to the high failure rate on the EWT and HSPT, several districts increased the number of basic skills teachers at the high school or added HSPT prep programs after school.

EARLY CHILDHOOD EDUCATION

All six special needs districts were committed to providing early childhood and full-day kindergarten programs in their communities. Three special needs districts (SN3, SN5, SN6) used QEA funds to dramatically expand their full-day kindergarten programs. Participation in full-day kindergarten increased between 60% and 350% in these communities; by 1993 the districts served 50% (SN5), 80% (SN3), and 100% (SN6) of their eligible students. Another district (SN4) already provided full-day kindergarten programs to all public school students prior to the enactment of the QEA. Only a lack of space prevented further expansion of the full-day kindergarten program in the communities that still did not provide full coverage.

Expansion of preschool services proceeded more slowly. District SN4 had a program of early childhood services in place prior to the QEA. This district had used its federal compensatory education funds to develop and house a half-day, 4-year-old program, and all interested students (about 55% to 60% of public school students) participated in this preschool program. Other children participated in Head Start or employer-provided day care programs. District SN2 had also initiated preschool services under the federal program, and QEA funds enabled the district to expand the program so that 85% of the district's children entered kindergarten with some preschool experience. Two more special needs districts (SN3, SN5) initiated or expanded small preschool programs using a combination of federal funds, QEA aid, and GoodStarts grants. But lack of funds and lack of space prevented them from expanding the programs further. The remaining two special needs districts in our study (SN1, SN6) had not initiated state-funded preschool programs by 1993/94 due, again, to lack of facilities or funds.

There is not much need for publicly funded preschool in the non–special needs districts in our sample. Most children in these communities participate in some kind of private preschool program before entering kindergarten. Only one non–special needs district in our sample provides a preschool program for nondisabled children. This small program serves students from low-income families in the community and is funded through the federal compensatory education program. Another district serves all of its students in a full-day kindergarten program, and three others had considered expanding their half-day kindergarten programs. Cost or lack of space has prevented them from doing so.

ALTERNATIVE SCHOOL PROGRAMS

The QEA enabled four special needs districts (SN1, SN3, SN4, SN5) to develop alternative programs for at-risk students who could not be served by the traditional school structure. Three programs served between 50 and 100 at-risk high school students, generally after school. The fourth program (SN5), located in a district with a large number of limited English-proficient and immigrant students, served 130 at-risk students in grades 4 through 9 and included a bilingual, port-of-entry class. This program had a waiting list of another 100 students.

AFTER-SCHOOL PROGRAMS

All six special needs districts developed or expanded after-school programs that provide a combination of curricular and extracurricular activities. District SN3, for example, established Homework Centers in its elementary schools to provide homework support for 2 hours, three afternoons a week. The program served over 4,000 students in 1992/93, the height of the QEA funding. Funding constraints forced a curtailment in services in 1993/94, and the program was eliminated totally in 1994/95. Some of these activities were picked up in the district's smaller Extended Day Program, which provided a wide range of services in a smaller number of schools. This program, which included before- and after-school activities, a breakfast program, tutoring, and programs and clubs for the students, was slated to become a "school-age child care program" with a fee based on a sliding scale to help cover costs. The district hoped to extend this program district wide.

District SN5 also initiated a fee-based after-school program for children 3 years of age through 4th grade. The $5/day fee was covered by the parent or by Welfare. The district planned to expand the program, which served 450 students in 24 schools (about 5% of all pre-kindergarten to grade 4 students in the district), to all elementary schools in the city.

Other districts had smaller and more-focused programs. SN4 started an after-school tutoring program for elementary school students in the first year of QEA. When the city took over this program, the district developed a Saturday parent/student science program. In SN6, a combination of local and federal drug prevention funds supported an after-school program in the middle schools. In SN2, after-school academic programs focused on the large number of ninth grade students failing two or more courses.

Although the majority of the special programs to meet the academic needs of students at-risk of school failure were concentrated in the special needs districts, and although most new program development during the period of our study took place in these districts, the foundation and transition aid districts also offered special programs for at-risk students. District staff were quick to point out that the non–special needs districts had at least some students at-risk, and they needed to provide for them.

Social Support Programs for At-Risk Students

All 12 districts, particularly the special needs districts, had been under pressure to provide programs and services to enhance the academic performance of students prior to the enactment of QEA. As we pointed out earlier, district staff were keenly aware of the performance of their students on the state-mandated assessment and responded by trying to find ways to boost student academic performance. With the advent of QEA, much of the effort in the special needs districts went into expanding social services for their students. The major changes in our case study districts included (1) expanding counseling and social work services, (2) expanding health services, (3) expanding school breakfast programs, and (4) developing outreach and support programs for parents. These programs were often designed to respond to social needs, both those internal to the school and those connected to the larger community.

COUNSELING AND SOCIAL WORK SERVICES

The QEA enabled the special needs districts to expand the number of counselors, social workers, and psychologists serving their students. Four special needs districts in our sample increased the number of social workers and psychologists serving their students by at least 50%. Among non–special needs districts, only FN1 increased the number of staff in this category, responding to its large enrollment growth.

Respondents in all six special needs districts reported using QEA funds to expand the number of counselors in their districts, especially in the elementary schools. By 1993/94, all the elementary schools in SN2, SN4, and SN5 had full-time counselors, as did all but four elementary schools in SN6. Prior to the QEA, there were no elementary counselors in SN4, and only part-time counseling services in the schools in the other districts. Funds were also used to provide additional substance abuse counselors (SAC) in the middle and high schools, special crisis intervention counselors, home/school liaisons, and bilingual counselors.

District SN3 took a more holistic approach to the provision of social services at the elementary school level with the creation of ten schools following the Comer (1996) model as we noted in Chapter 3. The Comer model is designed to address the underlying social and psychological processes of schooling. These approaches respond both to internally and externally based student needs for social support.

EXPANDING HEALTH SERVICES

The special needs districts recognized the necessity to expand support services to include the coordination of health and social services. Three districts (SN1, SN3, SN4) had pilot School-Based Youth Services (SBYS) schools, involving three of these districts' four high schools and one middle school. The SBYS programs, initiated prior to QEA, have been deemed very successful by staff. The high school center in SN4, for example, coordinated a range of health and social services for adolescents. Its middle school program worked with both students and their families.

As a result of the early successes of the coordinated services approach, the special needs districts were anxious to expand such coordinated social services to other schools. SN3 used QEA funds to establish a SBYS-type center in another high school. This district wanted to incorporate medical services in its K–8 schools moving to the Comer model but was constrained by the high cost of providing health services. Similarly, SN4 proposed creating SBYS centers in its elementary schools. A proposal to place school-based health clinics in grades K to 4 was received favorably by the state, but was not funded when the governor would not support an expansion of the SBYS program beyond the initial pilot sites.

COMMUNITY OUTREACH

Three special needs districts added community outreach programs to their mix of social service programs. In SN3 parent involvement in schooling increased through the establishment of Parent Centers and Parent Coordinators at both the district level and in eleven schools. The Parent Centers provided multiple services: job training and counseling; training in parenting skills, nutrition, or computers; GED programs; social activities, such as arts and crafts; and programs that familiarize parents with school curricula. Parents were encouraged to volunteer in the school, and to get involved in school activities, whether during the day or before and after school. The goal was to increase parent involvement with their children and their children's schoolwork, and to provide parents with a better understanding of what schools do for and with children. These centers were also locations for grassroots community building. The Parent Coordinators supervised the Parent Centers, coordinated their activities and programs, and served as a liaison between the schools and families. SN2 and SN5 offered the EPIC program (Effective Parenting Information for Children). In SN2, this program was offered on Saturday mornings in an attempt to combat child abuse, teenage pregnancy, juvenile crime, and alcohol and drug abuse.

SCHOOL BREAKFAST PROGRAMS

A final trend across the six special needs districts was an expansion of the school breakfast program. This program was started or expanded in most districts after 1990. Two districts (SN4, SN6) offered free breakfasts to all eligible students, and the others were moving in that direction.

Overall, although the special needs districts had attempted to meet the social needs of students in the years prior to the QEA, after its passage these districts expanded their efforts. Particularly notable was their growing capacity to respond to student social needs emanating outside the school.

Summary

The special needs districts in our sample, and statewide, used new funds generated by the QEA to expand their limited programs for at-risk students. The major targets were full-day kindergarten, supplemental academic programs (especially extended-day programs and alternative schools), counselors and other social service personnel, and school breakfast programs. Within the constraints of space and money, the districts also sought to increase preschool programs, health services, and programs for parents. Some goals have been met in some districts, particularly the smaller communities in our study. Two districts provide both half-day preschool and full-day kindergarten to most or all eligible students; most of the districts have a full-time counselor in every school; and most of the eligible students now have access to both free breakfast and lunch programs.

REMAINING CHALLENGES

Much remains to be done to address the special needs of at-risk students, however. Four special needs districts do not provide all students with a full-day kindergarten program, and these communities have no, or very limited, preschool programs. The two districts with half-day preschool programs want to expand these programs to the entire day and begin to enroll 3-year-old students. Both space and money are major barriers. Schools are overcrowded, and state regulations limit the use of alternative facilities. Even if space was available, the districts lack the funds needed to initiate these new programs. When the GoodStarts program first provided seed money for preschool programs in 1992/93, it was intended that the QEA would pick up the funding for these classes the following year, when these preschool children would be counted as part of the district's total enrollment. The GoodStarts money could then be "rolled over" to initiate still more classes. This strategy was never implemented, however, because the enrollment counts used to calculate QEA funding were frozen at their 1992/93 levels. Therefore no new state aid dollars were generated to cover the costs of preschool classes formed after 1992/93.

Although the districts have increased the number of counselors in their schools, there is a need for still more, especially to work with limited English-proficient students and to address drug and alcohol abuse and family problems. While the special needs districts in the sample now have, on average, twice as many school psychologists and social workers per 1,000 students as the wealthy suburban communities, the level of staffing—only 2 for every 1,000 students—is still inadequate when 50% to 80% of the urban students are at-risk of failing in school. Additional counseling services are provided by other programs, such as Weed and Seed, SBYS, and social service agencies, but these services are limited to a handful of schools and are insufficient to serve all the students who need help.

After-school programs and health services are still very limited. After-school programs funded in the early years of the QEA were cut back, or districts imposed parent fees, when state aid was no longer sufficient to pay for the programs. The expansion of school-based health and social services stalled due to the high costs of these services and the decision not to increase state support of the SBYS program. As a result, many high schools, and most elementary and middle schools in the urban districts lack sufficient health and social services.

The high-income districts in our sample face different needs and challenges. Here the challenge is one of attitude, not resources. These communities have a small, but growing number of at-risk children, most of whom are from low-income families or are members of racial/ethnic minority groups. While these communities have many support services in place, such as extensive counseling programs, teachers and administrators often seemed unsure of how to meet the needs of these at-risk students. A respondent in one wealthy community noted, "The district runs a college-prep program. This makes it very difficult to meet the needs of economically disadvantaged children whose families are in turmoil." Some respondents in two of the districts favored placing at-risk students in separate programs, and even in separate facilities. In one community, a vocal group of minority parents forced the district to initiate programs, such as a Saturday Parents Institute, to address the interests of minority parents, an after-school group to promote self-esteem among minority students, and an after-school tutoring program at the middle and high schools.

Middle-income districts are caught in the middle. As the number of at-risk children grows, these districts are often forced to reduce services designed to assist students at risk. FN2, for example, cut its summer school, parenting, after-school tutoring, and work experience programs due to budget constraints. It has maintained a full-day kindergarten program, but has had to drop plans for a preschool program due to lack of funds.

It is clear that the vast differences in the social conditions from which students come place quite different burdens on districts. For special needs districts serving large proportions of students at risk of school failure, these burdens are substantially greater than in other districts. The supreme court recognized this in its ruling in *Abbott*. The provisions of the QEA took this into account. The special needs districts responded by investing some of the additional resources provided through the QEA in programs designed precisely to address the special academic and social needs of their students. Although non–special needs districts do serve some students at risk of school failure, the cost to them of meeting the needs of limited numbers of such students does not compare to the considerable burdens placed upon special needs districts by large numbers of these students.

CONCLUSIONS

The social conditions in the communities from which the special needs districts draw their students developed over a long period of time as part of the general decline in the economic well-being of cities in New Jersey and elsewhere. These depressed social conditions cannot be rectified quickly, and their deleterious effects on students and their learning cannot be easily overcome. The QEA itself was not designed to address these issues fully though the decision of the New Jersey Supreme Court envisioned the need to do so. We lack good estimates of exactly what would be necessary to fulfill the educational needs of large concentrations of poor children. Nevertheless, in the wake of the QEA local school districts did make some progress.

The districts in our case studies did develop and implement new programs to respond to the special academic and social needs of their students. The funds made available through the QEA allowed the special needs districts to mount distinct efforts to create conditions to allow students to devote effort to their education and to provide special instructional opportunities and settings to facilitate their academic development.

But the progress spawned by the QEA was only a first step toward the kind of sustained effort required to reverse decades of educational decline in the special needs districts. Moreover, the special needs districts and their students remain under continued pressure from the social conditions in their communities, conditions that in some cases are becoming worse. Special efforts on the part of school districts are important, but renewed efforts to revive the social and economic bases of these communities, efforts that extend well beyond the schools, are key components in any serious strategy to improve the educational prospects for these students.

7
FACILITIES: DEFERRED MAINTENANCE, DEFERRED DREAMS

Meeting the special needs created by the social conditions in which students in the poor school districts live often entailed efforts to bring social programs of various sorts into the schools as the previous chapter detailed. However, the poor school districts typically have overcrowded or inadequate facilities for the basic educational program, even without additional programs to address the social needs of students. Thus, the constellation of problems long faced by the special needs districts continues to make it difficult to address the needs of poor children. The years of deferred maintenance and the limited capacity of poor districts to add to their physical facilities in response to growing enrollments meant that addressing facilities needs was an issue in all of the special needs districts and a priority in those where there was simply no space to house additional services for children.

But space to house new programs was only one facilities problem facing the districts in our sample. Buildings in special needs districts are old, in disrepair after years of deferred maintenance, and without adequate infrastructures to support computers and other new technologies. Suburban districts are searching for ways to house growing enrollments, and their schools, built during the baby boom years of the 1950s and 1960s, are now at the point of needing major renovations. In this chapter, we identify the scope and nature of the facilities problems in the years preceding the Quality Education Act (QEA) and the kinds of funding the state provided to address these problems, describe how our districts responded to their facilities needs, and discuss the challenges that remain.

NATURE OF THE PROBLEM

All six special needs districts in our study faced severe facilities problems. State studies, the reports of external review teams, and data presented to the courts in the *Abbott* litigation, all pointed to the same set of issues. First, buildings were exceedingly old. In one special needs district in our case study sample, 21 out of 38 buildings had been built before World War II. In another district 22 of 34 were of this vintage.

These districts were typical of urban school systems in New Jersey. A survey of school buildings throughout the state reported that 41% of the state's buildings were over 50 years old, an age at which maintenance costs begin to escalate. The bulk of the rest had been built in the 1950s and 1960s with an intended 30-year lifespan; they, too, needed major service. The cost of addressing these problems statewide was estimated at nearly $6 billion in repairs, renovations, and new construction (McAtee & Thomas, 1992).

While facilities problems were endemic, they were substantially worse in the special needs districts. This same state survey reported that 64% of buildings in the 30 special needs districts were more than 50 years old. Almost as many buildings had been built before the turn of the century (35), as had been constructed in the 1980s (43). In contrast, only 30% of the schools in wealthy suburban communities had been built before World War II (McAtee & Thomas, 1992).

Nor are New Jersey school districts alone in their failure to address major facilities deficiencies. The General Accounting Office (GAO) concluded that most U.S. schools are unprepared for the facilities demands of the 21st century in critical areas. Noting that 40% of schools have facilities that cannot meet the functional requirements of laboratory science or large-group instruction even moderately well, the GAO estimates that the cost of repairing and upgrading school facilities nationwide is $112 billion. Moreover, the authors of the GAO study pointed out that schools in central cities and those with 50% or more minority populations are likely to have larger numbers of unsatisfactory environmental conditions than other schools (General Accounting Office, 1995a, 1995b).

It is difficult to appreciate fully the age of many schools in the special needs districts. One paragraph in the state report captures it best:

> More than 130 years ago Abraham Lincoln made a whistle stop in New Jersey on his way to Washington, DC to be inaugurated. He spoke to children who attended the city's finest new schools from the train station's platform. Today, some of those same schools, so progressive in Lincoln's day, still house the city's school children. (McAtee & Thomas, 1992, p. 4)

These old buildings created a drain on the poor districts. As one administrator in charge of facilities noted, "All those old buildings are difficult to
keep up with all the youngsters we have." In several districts, there were
large numbers of code violations, resulting in part from sheer age. These violations figured prominently in the reports of the external review teams assem-
bled by the state to recommend how special needs districts should spend
new funds.

These conditions were caused by a lack of local funds, insufficient state
aid, and community resistance to bond issues. According to one maintenance supervisor:

> Maintenance should be 5% to 10% of the budget. It costs a fortune any time
> you touch something. My budget includes $1 million for capital projects in
> a district this size. Our total budget is $240 million. Maintenance is $2 mil-
> lion to $3 million. It's almost all salaries. Where do you get materials? That's
> why you have to bond, and bonding affects taxes. The mayor doesn't want
> to fix what you have.

Not surprisingly, principals in this district complained that maintenance
and repairs were slow and shoddy. In spite of these problems, gaining public
support for substantial repairs was difficult. Administrators in almost every
urban district in this study either told about bond issues that had been voted
down or how they were simply convinced that any efforts to get additional
funds to improve buildings would fail.

A second issue confronting the poor urban districts is that their students appear to be hard on the old buildings, a point noted in Chapter 4. The
fragile nature of systems in older buildings and the demands placed on facilities by students combine to make the maintenance task particularly challenging. As the maintenance director of one special needs district reported:
"In an urban area, everybody looks for schedules, but your normal day is emer-
gencies: heating problems, electrical problems, who clogged this?"

Third, urban schools did not provide enough space or the modern facilities needed to house the range of academic and social programs that are
part of a "thorough and efficient" education. In SN2, for example, 7 of 11 schools
were built before 1908 and an eighth dated from the 1920s. The state external review team report written to guide planning for this district noted that:

> The most critical problem faced by [SN2] schools and the most pressing pri-
> ority is the replacement and/or improvement of all school facilities.... In
> many schools wooden floors are warped and there is poor lighting, peel-
> ing paint, outdated heating plants, poor bathroom facilities, poor ventila-
> tion and need for control of pests. Elementary schools lack basic core facil-
> ities and there is a lack of classrooms or space for ESL classes, basic skills

> classes, libraries, music, art, physical education, computer labs. . . . Classes
> are often interrupted by individuals or groups who must walk through class-
> rooms because the buildings were designed without corridors. (New Jersey
> State Department of Education, 1990)

These problems plagued other urban communities as well.

Judge Lefelt documented the inadequacy of science facilities, libraries, computer centers, and physical education facilities in many special needs districts in his Office of Administrative Law decision in the *Abbott* case (*Abbott v Burke* 1988, OALDKT):

> There are few true science classrooms in Camden High School. The major-
> ity of the rooms used for science are regular classrooms that are used for
> biology, chemistry and physics. Facilities for hands-on experiments are not
> available. The laboratory tables in one science class are over 50 years old;
> there are no safety showers and no ventilation hoods. . . . When laboratory
> facilities do exist in urban districts they are more likely to be older, built
> in the 1920s and 1930s when the prevailing concept was that the teacher did
> the experiments and the students watched. (pp. 150–151)

> Of 24 elementary schools in Camden, 16 had no libraries. . . . As of 1984,
> Paterson had no libraries in any of its 30 elementary schools. . . . By con-
> trast, South Orange/Maplewood provides a librarian in each elementary
> school four days a week. (p. 186)

> One impediment to developing computer education in urban districts is that
> start-up costs are necessarily higher when there are more students in the
> district. . . . For example, both Ridgewood and Newark spent about the same
> for computer education in 1983. However, the $132,000 spent by Ridgewood
> meant all of its 5,100 students were given some access to a computer. The
> $120,000 spent by Newark gave only 1% of its 58,000 students computer
> access. . . . Another problem in urban districts is lack of adequate space for
> computer laboratories, since many facilities are already overcrowded. (pp.
> 142–143)

> [Physical education] facilities in urban districts tend to be older and in poor
> repair. Limits on space mean more students use the space at the same time;
> therefore activities are limited to those which can be done by large groups
> of students. . . . The director of Irvington High's PE program noted that stu-
> dents become disruptive out of boredom and frustration with "spending 20
> minutes each gym period waiting to take just one layup shot." (p. 165)

Finally, in half the special needs districts in our case studies, the facilities problems were compounded by enrollment growth. As discussed in Chapter

4, three of the six special needs districts experienced student enrollment increases of 6% or higher between 1990 and 1993. Even where growth was not a problem, overcrowding was. When asked if the QEA had allowed districts to reduce class sizes, the most typical response in all districts was that it was impossible to hire new teachers because there was no place to put them. In SN1, the lack of adequate facilities had all the buildings bursting at the seams. Grade-level configurations in the schools were a function of available space, not program philosophy. In SN4, the district used libraries and basic skills resource rooms to house its growing elementary school enrollments. The district could not expand the number of special education classes because of lack of space.

While the situation was not as extreme in the middle-income districts, they, too, experienced space constraints, although for different reasons. FN1 serves a fast growing, fringe suburban area. During the 1980s, it built five new schools. In the last half of that decade, its student population increased by 22%. This growth continued during the study period, albeit more slowly with the number of students increasing 10% between 1990 and 1993. Thus, classroom space was always an issue.

Growth was less of an issue in FN2; the district student body only increased 3% during the three years of the study. The problem there was more political. During the two decades preceding the passage of QEA—including periods of notable growth—district voters failed to pass any bond issue. In fact for the four years preceding QEA, voters would not pass a school budget, with fiscal conservatism growing constantly over the period. The construction that took place came through lease-purchase agreements. Because of the difficulty in arranging even lease-purchase agreements, buildings were sometimes small and inadequate. Some schools in the older part of town, which borders one of the state's cities, were old, outdated, and poorly designed. Class sizes were large because of failure to build in the past.

The buildings in the wealthier districts were in fundamentally better shape than those in the other districts. Most were newer than those in the poor districts. Many, like the high school in TR3, which has an elegant cafeteria with steam-table carts and striped canopies over a separate salad bar, echoed the modern malls that surrounded them. Some of the older buildings were quite well maintained and had been beautifully renovated. The middle school in TR2, with its graceful exterior stonework, beautiful auditorium, and pile-carpeted offices for the district administration, was a case in point.

Still, the four wealthy districts had some facilities problems. Three of the four experienced student population increases of 9% or more during the study period. Complaints about increasing class size were frequent, although these were sometimes about elementary classes going from 18 to 20 students. Still, at least two districts expanded facilities either just before or during the study period. The one district (TN4) that did not grow faced the problems of old buildings that typified poorer districts. A Middle States evaluation of this district's high school identified a number of problems, like faulty wiring, that needed to be addressed.

SOURCES OF FUNDING

State policy makers did not intend to fund major facilities projects through the QEA formula. The QEA did not change state aid for debt service, which allocated $78.5 million to school districts to offset debt incurred through school construction bonds. The QEA did replace a small ($14.5 million) capital outlay program with a $113 per pupil facilities component in the foundation level. Districts could use the $42 million of foundation aid generated by this component to address maintenance backlogs or they could bank these funds in a special Capital Reserve Account for use in future years.

To address larger construction needs, the Florio administration introduced a bill to create a $600 million facilities bond grant program. This initiative died in a legislative committee, however, in 1991. A year later, the legislature established four school facilities–funding programs totaling $300 million. The first program made $50 million in grants to special needs districts. All 30 special needs districts were entitled to receive these one-time grants if they had a spending plan approved by the SDE and could spend or encumber the funds by June 1994. The Safe Schools Loan Program ($25 million) enabled any school district in the state to bring facilities into compliance with health and safety code requirements, while the Public School Facilities Loan Program ($125 million) provided support for these and other school construction projects, ranging from repair and renovation to new construction. Repayments of these two low-interest (1.5%) loans, which covered 25% to 50% of the cost of the projects, were treated as net debt service for state aid purposes. The Small Projects Loan Program was a $100 million loan pool for public school projects that did not exceed $5 million in total cost, and could be used by local districts to borrow the balance of funds needed for either Safe Schools or Public School Facilities projects. The 30 special needs districts received all $50 million of the grants and $40 million from the three statewide loan funds, giving them a total of $90 million in facilities grants and loans.

THE DISTRICTS ADDRESS THEIR FACILITIES NEEDS

These state aid funds, when coupled with increases in general operating aid and successful bond referenda, led to a flurry of building activity during the

QEA years. All six special needs districts addressed facilities needs. Working with the city government, SN1 arranged for a $50 million bond issue to build one new school and make additions and various other substantial changes in others, including the high school. SN2 substantially increased its regular maintenance budget, arranged a $43 million lease-purchase, and also passed a $32 million bond issue to gut and rebuild the district's two middle schools as well as make substantial renovations and upgrades to its elementary schools. SN3 received $11 million from the state facilities programs to make additions to two elementary schools and repairs in the high schools. The district used about $8 million from its operating budget to do everything from replace chalkboards to bell systems to stairways and gym floors as well as put in new computer and science laboratories and elementary libraries.

SN4 used nearly $8 million in state facilities aid and loans to build 23 new elementary classrooms, make renovations in 2 elementary schools, and repair the roofs of 3 schools. In addition, the district levied $3.6 million in bonds to make renovations at the high school and to bring all school buildings up to code. Operating funds were used to build a new media center in 1 elementary school, and upgrade science and computer labs in the high school. SN5 received authorization from a special capital projects board and the city council to raise bond funds and did so on a case-by-case basis. Between 1990 and 1993, the district completed one new building and started a second to replace existing schools. It also made extensive renovations to 2 elementary schools and 2 high schools as well as building early childhood education facilities in housing projects. The district also replaced roofs, added libraries, and made a number of additional repairs. SN6 approved a $23 million bond issue that was used to renovate its high school. Almost all the districts addressed a variety of code violations and safety concerns that, while not dramatic in themselves, made the schools much less dangerous places for students to attend.

Four factors explain why the urban districts undertook these major efforts to upgrade their facilities after years of neglect. First, although the QEA formula itself provided little new money for facilities, increases in state aid coupled with the operation of the budget caps reduced school tax rates in several urban communities. In SN4, for example, the school tax levy dropped nearly 20% in the 2 years of the QEA. This gave the superintendent the opportunity to seek voter support for bond referenda without having to raise taxes above the 1990 level.

Second, the reports prepared by the external review teams highlighted building and facilities problems in the districts and gave superintendents and their boards the ammunition they needed to push for facilities referenda.

Third, the four grant and loan programs gave the districts needed money. The $50 million in grants to special needs districts, which were part of the 1993/94 school aid appropriation, did not have to be repaid. The districts had to repay the other $40 million dollars in loans, but the availability of the money, and the state requirement that the money be committed in 1993/94, gave the districts additional leverage to gain voter support of facilities bonds. In addition, districts received state debt service aid starting in 1994/95 to offset some of the cost of these loans.

A final factor was the foresight and leadership of the districts' superintendents and school boards. The leaders of these six districts identified facilities needs as a major district priority upon the passage of the QEA, and drew up plans for facilities renovations and construction almost immediately. SN4, for example, took a $9.3 million maintenance and building referendum to its voters in December 1991. After a surprising 2 to 1 defeat of this plan, the district returned to the voters with a pared down, $3.6 million maintenance referendum that was approved. When the state facilities grants and loans became available the next year, the district gave the state its unfunded facilities plans and garnered almost $8 million in grants and loans from the state.

SN2 also took an aggressive approach to building renovations. It was one of the better managed urban districts in the state known for its ability to develop effective instructional approaches. A state official familiar with SN2 described it as "a good district. It is very ambitious and wants to expand." Yet, the district could not move ahead programmatically until it addressed the facilities problems that had plagued it for decades. The district began to address the problem immediately. When the state awarded it $1 million in discretionary money in 1991/92, the administration devoted $750,000 to renovations at the middle school. Yet, grants of this size and reallocations within the regular operating budget could not begin to address the fundamental facilities problem.

The superintendent who directed SN2 into the first year of QEA had been a local resident who worked very closely with the city government. For all of his efforts to improve programs in previous years, he had avoided the facilities issue to forestall conflict with the city government, which opposed raising taxes further for schools. When he retired in 1991, however, his successor chose to take on the issue and proposed both a $43 million lease-purchase agreement that the board could authorize and a $32 million bond issue that had to be approved by the voters. This strategy was opposed by the mayor, who ran an opposing slate of candidates in the spring 1992 school board election to stop the building program. The superintendent actively campaigned for the incumbents, who won; voters approved the bond issue later that year.

Although all the special needs districts in our case studies identified major facilities needs and although leaders in all six districts initiated action to address those needs, they were not equally effective in making progress. In contrast to districts such as SN2 that made major progress, efforts to address facilities problems in SN1 and SN6 lagged notably behind the other urban districts. At the end of the 1993/94 school year, the county superintendent overseeing SN1 was using building code violations and monitoring standards to pressure the district to take drastic action to improve its high school. The building was so overcrowded and in such disrepair that he threatened to close it down for the last three weeks of the school year. SN6 could not mount an effective building plan despite the $23 million bond issue it had passed.

Although most construction took place in the poor districts in our sample, work was also underway in the other districts, most notably the two middle-income districts. FN1 built a new middle school and 5 early childhood classrooms to house its rapidly expanding student population. The district also made significant repairs to its schools, replacing windows, repaving parking lots, and renovating high school science labs and science suites as well as 20 classrooms in one elementary school. It also found resources to put a new TV studio in the high school. In spite of community opposition, FN2 arranged another lease-purchase to add 14 classrooms, in some cases to eliminate portable units, and fix rooms that were below code. These were mostly in the district's oldest high school.

Two wealthy districts also made significant upgrades, although in one case the work was initiated by a bond referendum voted before QEA passed. That district (TR1) built a new high school to consolidate two separate buildings into one. It also upgraded one wing of an elementary school, replaced underground storage tanks, and converted boilers in the old high school. TR3 put a new wing on its K–3 elementary school, repaired roofs, and made a variety of other changes. These improvements were funded through a combination of a voter-approved bond issue and a voter-approved waiver to the state-imposed spending cap. The two other wealthy districts made only small changes. Sometimes the speed with which repairs were made was reduced by lack of community support, but they still got done. For instance, when voters refused to pass a bond issue to support necessary improvements in TR4, the board of education voted to devote $1 million of its budget each year for 5 years for such major repairs. The money came from savings accrued by privatizing the maintenance function.

REMAINING CHALLENGES

In the 3 years following the passage of the QEA, the poor urban districts took major steps to upgrade their school facilities. The middle-income districts in our study also addressed their facilities needs, although not to the same extent. Yet, much remains to be done before urban schools will be comparable to those in the wealthy suburban communities.

The state has not published data on how much it will cost to address years of deferred maintenance, replace dilapidated schools, ease overcrowding, provide facilities that can support modern curriculum and new technology, and house programs for preschool and special needs students in New Jersey's urban districts. As the 30 special needs districts enroll one-quarter of the state's students, a conservative estimate of the cost of addressing facilities needs is one-fourth of the total state bill, or $1.5 billion. However, given the older age and poorer condition of urban schools, as noted by McAtee and Thomas (1992), the cost is probably considerably higher.

In an attempt to develop a more classroom-based measure of the facilities gap between the poor urban and wealthy districts in our sample, we collected information on the availability and quality of selected instructional facilities during our site visits and surveyed teachers in 62 schools in the 12 districts. In addition, we asked district administrators to identify the major facilities needs in their districts. Table 7.1 shows how teachers rated the adequacy of eight aspects of the physical environment of their classrooms

TABLE 7.1. *Mean teacher rating of aspects of the physical environment of their classrooms and schools by district type*

ASPECT RATED	SPECIAL NEEDS		FOUNDATION		TRANSITION	
	MEAN	N	MEAN	N	MEAN	N
Room Cleanliness	3.25	1234	3.40	221	3.36[a]	387
School Cleanliness	3.10	1234	3.54	219	3.43[b]	392
Instructional Space	3.05	1218	3.27	223	3.44[c]	390
Condition of Basic Systems	3.02	1231	3.18	222	3.39[d]	387
Security	2.73	1227	3.20	273	3.62[e]	391
Teachers' Lounges	2.65	1224	3.05	222	2.83[f]	382
Teachers' Group Space	2.55	1219	2.63	222	2.69[g]	386
Response to Maintenance Requests	3.03	1220	3.38	222	3.64[h]	388

Responses: 1 = very poor; 2 = poor; 3 = adequate; 4 = very good; 5 = excellent.
[a] $F = 3.356, p < .05$
[b] $F = 31.153, p < .001$
[c] $F = 22.943, p < .001$
[d] $F = 23.012, p < .001$
[e] $F = 123.518, p < .001$
[f] $F = 15.838, p < .001$
[g] $F = 3.122, p < .05$
[h] $F = 59.318, p < .001$

and schools in the spring of 1994. Teachers were asked to comment on the cleanliness of their classrooms, the cleanliness of their schools, the adequacy of their instructional space, the condition of basic school systems, security, teachers' lounges, space for teacher group meetings, and responses to their requests for maintenance.

Teachers in the special needs districts generally rated these aspects of their physical environments as at least adequate, with the exception of security, teachers' lounges, and space for teacher group meetings, each of which was rated as between poor and adequate. Teachers in special needs districts rated each of the eight aspects of the physical environment lower than their counterparts in the foundation aid and transition aid districts. Teachers in the non–special needs districts rated these aspects of the physical environment as between adequate and very good with the exception of the teachers' lounges and teacher group meeting space, which were rated lower.

Direct observation as part of our site visits showed even more clearly the differences in facilities between the rich and poor school districts. As shown in Table 7.2, nearly half of elementary schools visited in special needs districts lacked art and music rooms and 40% of the middle schools visited in special needs districts lacked science labs.

Moreover, 40% of the libraries in schools visited in special needs districts were deemed inadequate, as were science labs in two of the seven high

TABLE 7.2. *Site visitor ratings of buildings and facilities by district type*

FACILITY	RATINGS	SPECIAL NEEDS		FOUNDATION AID		TRANSITION AID	
		N	%	N	%	N	%
Elementary art	Missing	10	48	4	80	1	14
and music rooms	Present	11	52	1	20	6	86
School library	Needs upgrade	13	41	2	22	2	14
	Adequate	14	44	7	78	11	79
	New/excellent	5	16	0	0	1	7
Middle school	None	4	40	0	0	0	0
science labs	Needs upgrade	1	10	1	50	0	0
	Adequate	5	50	1	50	4	100
High school	Needs upgrade	2	29	1	50	0	0
	Adequate	5	71	1	50	4	100
Other space	Need more	17	59	6	75	1	7
	Adequate	12	41	2	25	14	93

schools in these districts. In 59% of the schools, administrators reported they needed additional space to house academic or social support programs.

In contrast, only one elementary school that we visited in the transition aid districts lacked an art and music room. All the middle schools and high schools contained science labs and all were deemed adequate by their building principals. Of the 14 schools visited in the transition aid districts, only two had inadequate library space, and only one administrator reported needing additional space for educational programs. The situation for the foundation aid districts was generally better than the special needs districts though not as good as the transition aid districts with two exceptions: four of the five elementary schools in the foundation aid districts lacked art and music rooms, and administrators in six of the eight schools visited at all levels in these districts reported needing more space for academic or social support programs.

Reports from a member of our site visit teams who visited middle schools in both SN2 and TR2 reveal the striking contrast not only in facilities, but in the expectations regarding facilities in these very different kinds of districts. Describing an interview with an English as a second language teacher in the SN2 middle school, the site visitor wrote:

> We began our interview in the only available space in the school, a basement closet. This closet was approximately 8 feet wide by 10 feet long. The brick walls were painted eye-saving green, and the cement floors were painted grey, but there was no mistaking that this "room" without windows had previously been used to store materials. It was now used for a variety of things including instruction in basic skills for small groups of students. It was available for our interview, but only until the basic skills teacher arrived with a student.
>
> Asking the questions about facilities in this room prompted knowing smiles from the teacher who explained that the school had too little space for the regular classes let alone anything special. She insisted that I accompany her on a tour of the room in which she teaches following the interview.
>
> Later as we walked upstairs to her classroom the teacher explained that she taught in a room with two other teachers, each teaching a separate class. When we entered the classroom I discovered that it was a large room with a balcony level of sorts. One class was conducted on the upper level; two classes were being conducted on the main floor. There must have been 60 students in the room. A line of portable chalk boards placed end-to-end separated the two classes on the main floor. The teacher explained that the district had purchased dividers like those used in open space offices, but they were very flimsy and easily tipped over by students so the teachers had gone back to using the chalk boards. Students in the last row of each of the two classes sat with their backs to the room divider-chalk boards. I asked the teacher if having students from two different classes so close posed any

problems, and she replied that there were continuous problems with students talking and passing messages across the chalkboard barrier. Occasionally a student would lean back and tip over a chair and with it one of the chalk boards. She also added that it was difficult to conduct class when two other teachers could be easily heard, but she was getting used to it.

This same site visitor interviewed a teacher in the middle school in TR2 and received a very different response to questions about facilities:

> The TR2 middle school is old but has clearly been renovated and is well maintained. I conducted the interview in a brightly lit carpeted room with a full wall of windows. Each teacher in the English department had a desk in this room and used it for work and for meeting with students. . . . When I turned to the questions on facilities, the teacher reported that the facility was more than adequate and offered plenty of space for the entire school program. When I pressed her about any changes in facilities or maintenance following the passage of QEA, the teacher thought for a moment or two and then noted that "I think they may be washing the windows in my office a bit less frequently, but other than that I have seen no negative effects."

Clearly the physical conditions for schooling in these two middle schools differed dramatically. Both buildings were old, but the school in TR2 had been renovated and had sufficient room for a full range of programs. The school in SN2 was scheduled for complete renovation, but was overcrowded. Students and teachers in the SN2 middle school dealt daily with conditions that their counterparts in TR2 could not even imagine.

At the end of this study local districts faced three major challenges as they addressed continuing facilities needs: a lack of money, a lack of public support for facilities bond issues, and the pressures of continued enrollment growth.

Lack of Money

The facilities grants and loan programs enacted in 1992 provided much-needed funds for school districts, but the $90 million funneled to the special needs districts and the $143 million loaned to the non–special needs districts addressed less than 5% of the projected $6 billion dollar need. Raising additional facilities funds was particularly difficult for the urban districts, which lacked the tax base and the state aid to help them repay this round of loans. Although the facilities loans and other local facilities bond issues were eligible for state debt service aid, the state did not increase its appropriation for debt service aid accordingly in 1994/95. As a result, all districts eligible for debt service aid received only a portion of their expected aid. This aid reduction caused an unexpected rise in school tax levies in the special needs and foundation aid districts. If state debt service aid does not increase in the future, it will become even more expensive (and difficult) for districts to raise additional funds for facilities.

Lack of Public Support for Spending

In the past, public support for expenditures on facilities was highly correlated with the wealth of the district. This pattern has continued, but appears to be weakening. In four of the six special needs districts opposition to increased funding for schools was reflected in defeated budgets, defeated bond issues, and clear expressions of opposition from a city government that either controlled financial decisions or had substantial influence with the board and superintendent. One district where opposition was not reported was so poor that no one believed that finances for new buildings could be generated locally.

The situation was somewhat similar in the two middle-income districts. FN2 had a long history of opposition to bond referendums and by the end of the study period had defeated seven school budgets in a row. The other district had been more supportive of construction for its fast growing population, but by the time of the QEA, this support was waning.

The historically strong support for school funding in the richest districts was showing signs of crumbling. The only district that showed the strong support that had been typical of wealthy districts was TR2, where 450 people showed up to oppose cuts to the education budget proposed by the city government. In contrast, TR4, which had seen itself as competing with the elite private schools for students, found community support for education declining after 1987, partly in response to what were seen as lucrative contracts for teachers. A 1991 bond issue was defeated. Support for educational spending was also soft in the other two districts, but this seemed to reflect local opposition to questionable management decisions rather than deep-seated discontent.

Enrollment Growth

Growth in student populations and growth in specialized student programs will continue to place additional pressure on facilities in most of our study districts. Half the districts in our case studies experienced student growth of about 10% or more over the three years of the study. Two of these (SN1, SN5) were poor, one (FN1) was middle income, and three (TN1, TN2, TN3) were wealthy. Even in urban districts with lower overall growth, increasing demand for special education and bilingual/ESL services and for pre-kindergarten and full-day kindergarten programs required additional classroom space.

CONCLUSIONS

The distressed physical conditions of schools in the special needs districts developed over a long period of time. The distressed physical infrastructure with which these districts must contend cannot be rectified quickly. The estimates of the resources required to meet the physical plant needs of schools, particularly urban schools, dwarf any efforts to address them.

The local tax relief made possible by the QEA, together with other state support for facilities construction and improvement, allowed local districts to undertake major capital improvement plans. Improvement efforts of this magnitude were unthinkable in several special needs districts only a few years earlier. Still, the gap between rich and poor districts remains considerable. Further efforts to address the problem remain impossible with local resources alone. Improvements to infrastructure require continued support from the state if progress is to be sustained.

8

CONCLUSION

The previous chapters have traced in some detail the linkages between changed state finance and related policies and modifications of capacities to deliver education in rich and poor school districts. The central lesson of this exercise is that within the limits of New Jersey's specific equalization effort, increasing revenues for urban districts are generally translated into enhanced services and a more humane environment for the children in those schools. Yet, this translation process is a complex one, dependent on both central policy and local factors. Moreover, the story of this one state's effort at school finance reform is intricate; in fact, it is really three stories. We conclude by summarizing these stories and then suggesting implications for educational policy makers.

THE THREE STORIES OF SCHOOL FINANCE REFORM IN NEW JERSEY

The Quality Education Act (QEA) story has three parts. The first is the education story, the account of how the resources sent to poor districts by the new finance policy precipitated by the *Abbott* decision began to change students' educational opportunities. This story holds answers to two of our original research questions: did changed expenditures equalize districts' capacities to provide a quality education to students, and what other factors affected changes in those same capacities? The second story answers our third question about fiscal equalization by describing how resources changed in poor, middle-income, and wealthy school districts. Finally, there is the political story—the tale of how individuals and organizations embodying diverse interests responded to the passage of the QEA. This story goes beyond our research questions but tells a great deal about the feasibility of achieving a high quality education for all students. While these stories are about what happened in New Jersey, each also offers broader lessons for the many states currently involved in school finance reform.

The Education Story

The QEA and other finance reform policies designed to address inequities in educational resources have at their heart one fundamental goal: to provide equal educational opportunity to all students served by the public schools of a given state. As the testimony before the New Jersey Supreme Court in the *Abbott* case made clear, dramatic differences in resources among the many local districts of the state resulted in gross inequities in the educational opportunities afforded students. These inequities extended into all aspects of the schooling process, including the qualifications of school staff, the school curriculum, and facilities.

Our central educational question was whether and to what degree the QEA began to redress this situation. More specifically, in the wake of the QEA, did the poor school districts improve the educational opportunities afforded their students? Our answer is, in a word, yes. These urban districts improved the services they provided students. Beyond that, things become more complex as we show that some districts progressed more rapidly than others and identify factors to explain the differences. Finally, a large gap remained in educational services between rich and poor districts, even among the districts that made the most headway.

At the level of the simple provision of schooling resources, it is clear from both our case studies and our statewide survey data that leaders in the special needs districts used the additional resources made available under the QEA to improve the complex infrastructure that constitutes the opportunities for education in local school districts. The special needs districts used new funding to make long-needed investments in physical plant, educational personnel, the basic educational program, and more specialized services for students.

The physical plant improvements addressed years of neglect under budgets too lean to support even basic maintenance of facilities at levels mandated by health and safety codes. Because of the QEA, many fewer students in the special needs districts attend unsafe, inadequate schools. With regard to facilities, money made a difference.

The special needs districts also used QEA funds to hire additional personnel to staff basic programs and to provide additional services, although the changes were modest. The numbers of students involved were so large and the costs of personnel so high that major changes were simply precluded by the resources available. Moreover, some districts were cautious about hiring new professionals in view of the state's uncertain commitment to equalizing educational funding. Thus, while the changes were not as dramatic as in other areas, money also made a difference with regard to personnel.

The special needs districts used QEA funds to press forward with curriculum revisions in response to national and state movements for curriculum renewal. These curriculum revisions included raising standards and moving beyond the provision of just basic skills in line with the mandate of the state supreme court and the pressure of more challenging state tests. Our work illustrates how QEA funds allowed the special needs districts to improve curricula and provide necessary materials in ways that had previously been impossible. Moreover, staff received professional development to help them teach in ways that maximized the use of new materials and were more likely to promote student learning of more challenging content. Hence, for the basic academic program, money also made a difference.

Finally, the special needs districts used resources provided under the QEA to maintain existing and develop additional specialized programs for students and their families. These programs addressed the special needs of students in poor communities and families lacking the various, normally available resources of middle-class families. Such programs often make the difference between a student staying in school and succeeding or gradually failing and withdrawing. Thus money also made a difference in supporting students at risk.

While the QEA spelled progress for urban districts overall, some benefited from the new policy more than others. At least three factors helped some districts take the greatest advantage of new funding. One was changes in student enrollments. Three poor urban districts noticeably improved their ratios of professional staff to students while two actually lost ground. The difference was that the student population was essentially stable in the first three. In the other two, enrollment growth of 10% or more absorbed increased state funding.

The second factor was local political constraints. In two poor cities, the districts convinced their municipal governments and the public to combine increased state aid with unusual 1-year increases in local funding. In a third, the city government fought the state to get property taxes reduced as much as possible, severely limiting funding available for program improvement.

The third factor was the local district culture. Innovative districts have cultures that stress mutual trust and the primacy of educational services over bureaucratic or political concerns (Berman & McLaughlin, 1979). Among our poor urban districts, two out of six were notable for the absence of these characteristics. These were the ones that had trouble developing plans to take advantage of increased state funding and where progress in changing curricular and instructional approaches or expanding social services was particularly slow.

Was there some disorganization and less-effective planning in some special needs districts? Absolutely, but these instances were limited and found in predictable situations—internally divided districts with weak leadership that could not assess preexisting needs to develop an agenda to move forward. The instances of these events should not obscure the major finding that most districts most of the time were ready to use new funds provided by the QEA and could develop and implement plans despite the turmoil surrounding the passage and implementation of the law.

If the QEA spelled progress for poor urban districts, the gap between these and the state's wealthiest districts remained. Buildings improved, but they remained older and less well furnished than those in the richest suburbs. Some staff were added in the poor districts, but the substantial salary gap between rich and poor districts was essentially untouched, giving the former a distinct advantage in recruiting and retaining skilled professionals. Instructional programs improved, but the poor urban districts were just beginning to adopt new educational practices that had been in the suburban districts for several years. Finally, the poor urban districts expanded their social services, but the wealthy and even middle-income districts rarely needed to provide such services because they served areas with much stronger family organizations and greater social capital.

The Finance Story

The educational gap at the end of our study reflects the main finance story of QEA: the failure to achieve fiscal equity. Although the special needs districts did receive additional funds under the act and the gap between the poorest districts and the wealthiest districts did narrow, the disparity in the resources available in these different kinds of districts remained.

Several factors impeded the movement toward resource equity and equality of educational opportunity in the special needs districts. First, the additional resources made available under the QEA had to be used to redress the deficiencies that had developed over long years of underfunding. The special needs districts had extensive backlogs of physical plant problems and deferred maintenance. Second, districts used new resources to meet the special needs of at-risk students and their families, to provide a base of support so students could take advantage of the educational program. These funds supported programs in the academic areas as well as those designed to promote the health and welfare of students. As the court recognized in the *Abbott* decision, these needs are simply not as pervasive in the non–special needs districts. Third, costs in all districts increased due to growing enrollments, rising labor costs, and the growth in the numbers of students needing special educational services. Some new QEA funds were absorbed by these escalating demands on special needs districts' budgets. Fourth, the QEA oversight procedures demanded by the skeptical public exacted additional management costs in the special needs districts, costs that were exacerbated by the instability of state finance policy in the early nineties.

These impediments to the equalization of educational opportunities all concern the use of new funds. However, the greatest barrier to equity was the failure to provide an equal base of funding in the QEA itself. The reduction in state aid from the levels anticipated in the first QEA and the shifting of funds from support of the educational program to property tax relief were steps away from educational equity. Explaining that retreat from the initial plan takes us to the political story of educational finance reform in New Jersey.

The Political Story

The lack of will to achieve equity is the central theme of the political story surrounding the legislative response to the *Abbott* decision, the QEA. But there is more involved than just benign neglect or insufficient effort to bring about a legislative solution that would equalize spending statewide. State leaders in the end failed to act to achieve equity because of stubborn, hard-bitten opposition to distributing public resources equitably. Many individuals and groups fought publicly and zealously to continue to use the public schools and the public purse to maintain advantages for wealthy white communities, families, and children at the expense of poor non-white communities, families, and children. This was democracy in action.

The battle against the faithful execution of the clear intent of the state constitutional provision that all students be provided with a thorough and efficient education was waged on several levels, each of which reveals something about the battles that lie ahead in states confronting similar inequitable finance arrangements. The New Jersey case is particularly revealing because many of the participants in the public debate felt no sense of shame as they argued to maintain an inherently unequal system of public education in which public money was used to confer private privilege to students in their well-appointed suburban schools while basic health and safety standards were routinely violated in their underfinanced urban counterparts.

As we noted at the outset in Chapter 1, the arguments against school finance reform took several forms. First, some argued that the special needs districts were bottomless pits where additional state resources would only be squandered through waste and mismanagement. Part of this argument was the whispered claim that the students in these districts were not worth the investment because they would not learn anyway. Second, there was the accompanying contention that providing more money to the special needs districts required shifting funds away from the high-achievement suburban districts that served as lighthouses of excellence, models for their lesser city cousins. Proponents of this position maintained that when the lighthouse districts crumbled under the weight of the finance reform, these models of excellence would disappear and the state overall would be worse off. Curiously, swirling around at the same was a third argument: when it comes to schooling, money just does not matter. Of course none of those advancing this argument were willing to give up the resources they currently enjoyed.

More polite positions were taken by those who wished to maintain the sanctity of local control of schools and their resources. "Local control" provided the cover for the many residents of wealthy towns and communities who left the cities for their current homes and sought to leave urban problems behind. The battle over whether the state or local residents should set local spending levels surfaced in efforts by suburban legislators to amend the state constitution to remove the clause requiring the state to provide a thorough and efficient education to all students. The failure of this amendment to reach the floor of either house of the legislature should not conceal the extremes to which at least some state leaders (and presumably their supporters) were willing to go to avoid the equitable financing of the public schools of the state.

The issue re-emerged in the legislature in 1996. Governor Christie Whitman, who had defeated Florio on a tax reduction platform, still had to address the 1994 *Abbott* decision after reducing the state income tax rates by 30%. While the court called for the state to equalize regular education spending between the poor urban and wealthy suburban districts, the state had minimal control of spending decisions in the wealthy communities. Budget decisions are controlled by local voters and nearly all revenues are drawn from the local property tax. The Whitman administration addressed this problem by establishing a minimum spending level—a new foundation amount—that purported to provide sufficient revenues for all districts to meet the new state core curriculum content standards. This foundation amount became the administration's definition of a "thorough and efficient" education. Citizens would not have to vote on any education budget that matched this foundation level; however, spending above this amount would be labeled unnecessary to meet state standards and subject to a public referendum.

From the state's perspective, this strategy had two advantages over past funding formulas. First, it potentially set more stringent limitations on expenditures in the wealthy districts if voters chose not to support spending above the foundation amount. Second, it provided a rationale for not equalizing all spending in wealthy districts (the so-called excess costs, or local leeway spending). The proposed foundation level, however, was set considerably lower than expenditures in over half of the districts in New Jersey, with the wealthy suburban districts spending more than $200 million in local leeway spending (New Jersey Office of Legislative Services, 1996).

The administration's proposal created an uproar among parents and educators in the suburban districts who argued that this local leeway spending was necessary to provide an education at high standards and worried that subjecting this additional spending to a local vote would endanger existing curricula and programs. As a result, the legislature rejected the administration's plan. One legislator noted that "[w]e . . . wanted to make certain that high performing districts were not targeted for deep spending cuts under the guise of educational parity" (*New Jersey Assembly Republican News*, 1996).

IMPLICATIONS FOR THE THREE Es

The three stories of New Jersey's QEA provide a basis for reconsidering three major themes in American educational policy debates: excellence, efficiency, and equity.

Excellence

For at least a decade and a half now excellence has been seen, as Clune (1994) colloquially puts it, as providing "hard stuff for all kids" (p. 379). The constructivist revolution in thinking about teaching and learning has provided more refined definitions of what "hard stuff" should help American children become productive workers and citizens. Policy analysts and policy makers have suggested tougher and more comprehensive standards and approaches for mobilizing resources to achieve those standards.

Despite the substantial debates among educators and policy makers over what these standards should be, there is a major gap between this discussion and the problems that educators, especially those in urban districts, must face daily. The standards on which there is most consensus focus on what students should know. There is substantial agreement that such standards are necessary, especially in the traditional three Rs, although there is debate over how high they should be set (basic skills versus more complex problem solving), what range of subjects should be included, and what the stakes should be for students, teachers, and schools. There is considerably less agreement about whether there should be opportunity-to-learn standards specifying that curricula be aligned with student standards and that high-quality appropriate materials and adequately prepared teachers be made available to students before they are held accountable for what they learn. Proposals for the state and federal governments to mandate opportunity-to-learn standards have been hotly debated and largely defeated in the nineties.

Yet, from the perspective of urban school districts, the objects covered by opportunity-to-learn standards represent just a small part of the array of materials and services that must be provided if the children of the poor are to stay in school, much less learn the "hard stuff" now expected of them. In fact, training, materials, and aligned curricula turn out to be secondary needs in poor urban districts. Before children can benefit from "higher level" standards, they need safe settings with at least sufficient amenities to make learning a physically comfortable experience. Moreover, if good teachers are to stay in urban districts, they need the same things. Children who come to school with less social capital than their middle-class peers and competitors need special programs to help them develop that capital if they are to take advantage of more complex curricula and learn to more challenging standards. They also need similar numbers of teachers and administrators of comparable quality.

While our research does not in any sense "prove" that these conditions are prerequisites for poor children learning "hard stuff," we can say that educators in urban districts worry about providing these conditions and typically lack the resources to do so at the level available (through the schools themselves or through communities) in other areas. These observations of what urban districts do suggest that the excellence agenda ought to be expanded beyond a focus on student cognition and the most proximate technology (curriculum and instruction) for addressing it to truly address these more basic issues. Moreover, a budget for achieving excellence for all students ought to take these costs into account. Providing decent working conditions for poor children is not waste and mismanagement.

Efficiency

Much of the current talk about efficiency is based on the assumption that public schools are wasteful and worse, in part reflecting the dramatic increases in education costs over time. Studies examining expenditure patterns find little variation among districts, suggesting that it is difficult to attribute major waste to local mismanagement. Yet, these studies have rarely gone beyond financial data to see what money is buying. In this regard, our more qualitative approach based on direct observation and interviews and questionnaire data from educators on site provides a kind of information that has seldom been available before.

This work suggests two important conclusions. First, there are not obvious differences in efficiency between rich and poor districts. Most urban educators have a good sense of their own needs and ideas for addressing those needs. These educators, like those in other districts, know about new educational developments and assess the utility of those developments for their students. If the flow of new money to urban districts does not lead to dramatic changes in student performance, it is probably because urban educators want to make changes across a broad front, from facilities through materials to professional development on new approaches to instruction. By not concentrating funds in any one area, urban educators will make improvements in many of them, but none of these will be revolutionary.

Critics of increased spending might question the efficiency of focusing new dollars on noninstructional activities because there is no evidence relating, for example, new facilities to achievement. However, it is important to keep in mind that what the urban districts are doing is replicating what suburban districts have done over the years. The model for urban districts is what is done in suburban districts. By their actions suburban districts would maintain that modern, efficient buildings are a requirement. Urban and suburban educators are thus pursuing a common model of schooling. Moreover, it is this common model against which the state government is monitoring all districts.

Second, these data point to tradeoffs in some common policies central authorities use to help ensure local efficiency, although specific predictions will depend on the form these policies take in particular states. One of these is a strategy of limiting the amount of money that can be spent on education; in New Jersey, this was accomplished through spending caps that were set higher in poor urban districts than in others. The tradeoff here is that the same mechanism designed to reduce waste also limits the funds available for improved materials and services to students. In this regard, the "effect" of the policy will depend on each district's ability to develop a coherent, incremental improvement plan. Whether such a policy is useful depends on one's assessment of the typical district's ability to mobilize to improve its program. Given our observations on the reasonableness of most districts' use of new funds, the cap strategy limits useful program development more than it spurs efficiency. On the other hand, new state money not going to schools does address a different need: property tax relief. While this use was not educationally effective, the inequitably high local property tax rates in poor urban areas suggest that caps may be good tax policy even if they do not promote improved educational services.

Another tool to promote efficiency is to expand accountability. In New Jersey, this was done through a special oversight mechanism for the poor urban districts, and our work points to the tradeoffs in such policies. Intensive oversight does prevent gross mismanagement in the most inept districts, but it cannot facilitate the development of more than minimally acceptable plans for improvement. Moreover, such oversight adds (albeit minimally) to the management costs of those districts overseen, the effective and ineffective alike.

Thus, at best, it reduces efficiency in most districts that have reasonable approaches to improvement while only minimizing the grossest abuses in the few that do not.

Caps and oversight may contain the level of inefficiency in poor urban districts, but they do not promote efficiency. Efforts in that direction will require a substantial change in culture in the most divided and bureaucratic districts. Given the level of distrust between the state and local levels in New Jersey, it is hard to imagine the department of education playing a central role in such efforts.

More broadly, the conflict and distrust in the most dysfunctional districts we visited seem to reflect the social disorganization in the surrounding community. In these cities, many of the remaining residents fight each other for the crumbs of dying economies and lack the resources to move to more prosperous environments. The schools may be the most functional of the remaining institutions in these areas, in some cases even overcoming the limitations of their communities, but they are deeply influenced by the surrounding disarray. Anyon's (1997) history illustrating the connections between the decline of Newark's schools and the long-term decline of that entire city suggests that problems that have taken so long to develop will not be solved quickly and certainly not by the kind of policy Band-aids that New Jersey's regulatory strategy entailed.

Finally, in keeping with the political story, it is important to point out that there are levels of meaning and intent in cries to increase efficiency. At one level, the need to help educators become more efficient is real, although we suggest that that need is not limited to poor urban districts. At another, complaints about inefficiency reflect educators' limited success in showing how they can overcome the effects of family background on student achievement, suggesting that we need to find more efficient and effective ways to meet the needs of the nation's poor and minority students. These same complaints also reflect the current doubts about government's ability to address common problems and this country's extreme individualism (Bellah et al., 1985). As such, they are a cover for a growing unwillingness of Americans to accept responsibility for the well-being of all their fellow countrymen.

Equity

New Jersey's experience with school finance reform suggests reasons for optimism and pessimism about the litigation-based approach to promoting educational equity. On the one hand, this research suggests that, on balance, increasing expenditures in urban districts can improve the lot of poor urban children. Our work indicates that, at least within the limits of the New Jersey reform, increased funding will be used constructively.

Yet, at the end of this study, we are not encouraged about the likelihood of achieving equity for the nation's poor in the short or middle term. The gap between the rich and poor districts in this country continues to be dramatic in both what students bring to school and the services they receive when they arrive. This gap is maintained by the absence of political will. The litigation strategy has helped to minimize the damage to urban schools, but it has not bridged the gap between rich and poor. Twenty-five years of new court cases have generated stalled litigation and legislative steps forward followed by years of inaction with, at best, only minimal, often temporary, reductions in the inequities between rich and poor districts.

Litigation has not been effective largely because the political will to provide equal educational opportunity is simply not there. This will is undermined by a number of factors. First, school finance politics cannot be separated from the politics of race. New Jersey's poor and minority students are concentrated in cities that, because of their small and declining size, have limited power in the legislature. They are also targets of racial and social biases. The common belief that increasing expenditures in these districts will have little impact on students' achievement, in part, reflects such racism. For this reason, a formula designed to help only the urban districts will fail politically. To gain support for the poor urban districts, it is necessary to build alliances with the high- and middle-income districts whose representatives control the legislative agenda. Efforts to level down spending undermine such alliance building.

Equity is expensive and is tied to the politics of taxation. Building support among nonurban districts by equalizing up usually raises taxes. That angers a different constituency. Governor Florio's mistake was leading with tax changes rather than educational changes. This strategy was fiscally necessary given the condition of the economy and the state's finances at the time, but it proved to be politically suicidal.

If there is a way out of the box created by taxpayer resistance and lack of voter support for educational equity, it is by linking revisions in school finance formulae to broader educational reform. Increased state aid may be more palatable if it is linked to measures that change the substance of education: new educational standards, new assessments, and the like. Such measures may demonstrate to a wary public what new funds will buy.

While such an approach is promising if used to promote equity and excellence simultaneously, something very similar to it can be used to avoid addressing the equity problem. The Whitman administration proposed substituting equity in standards of student achievement for equity in fiscal inputs. It argued that fiscal equity does not matter if all students are held to the same standards, an argument that was subsequently rejected by the court. Such a strategy might have promise if it were linked to some plan for opportunity-to-learn standards that specified what curricular and social conditions must be in place before students can be held accountable for learning some specific content. In the absence of such standards and an understanding that the state and local districts are jointly accountable for ensuring that opportunities to learn are present, tougher standards can become a new, more sophisticated way of blaming the victim, in this case New Jersey's poor urban students. Addressing the equity and excellence problems efficiently requires a combination of fiscal and educational policy intended to address the needs of all students, especially the poor and minorities in a spirit of hope and trust in the potential of all our students. It will not be served by strategies to use standards and curriculum reform to avoid finance reform.

A CALL FOR RESEARCH AND A CALL FOR ACTION

Despite our doubts about the larger political context, there remains an important role for research to play. This is one of the first studies that has attempted to mesh the questions and methods of school finance research with those used to study policy implementation and changes in educational practice. We are impressed with what a complex, difficult process such research can be. Yet, to understand better how money can make a difference (and the kind of difference that it can make), we need more studies that look simultaneously at revenues, expenditures, local decisions, and educational practice. The linkages between expenditures and instruction are loose partly because there are many ways to spend money, both well and poorly. After all, education is a process that comes from interactions among teachers, students, and the content taught; and such interactions are only affected indirectly by funding. There is a great deal of room to learn more from studies that follow changed finance policies into classroom (and on-site social service centers). At the same time, we need to do a better job of calculating costs of efforts to raise standards and otherwise change practice.

Yet research alone is not enough. Research can show the need for certain kinds of policies and help provide answers to questions of policy design, but such knowledge is useful only if there is a willingness to act on it. For research (or practice) to improve policy, there must be an audience of receptive political leaders who hold that improving educational opportunity for the nation's poor is both a possibility and a responsibility. Such leaders are likely to appear only when the public is confident of its future and generous in its view about what this country should do for its least advantaged people.

REFERENCES

Abbott v Burke, 100 N.J. 269 (1985). (*Abbott I*)

Abbott v Burke, 119 N.J. 287 (1990). (*Abbott II*)

Abbott v Burke, 136 N.J. 444 (1994). (*Abbott III*)

Abbott v Burke. (1988). OALDKT, NO. EDU 5581–85.

Airasian, P. W. (1991). *Classroom assessment*. New York: McGraw Hill.

Anderson, B., and Pipho, C. (1984). State-mandated testing and the fact of the local control. *Phi Delta Kappan, 66*(3), 209–212.

Anderson, C. (October 1, 1995). N.J.'s other ways to give kids good start. *Trenton Times*, p. A7.

Anyon, J. *Ghetto schooling: A political economy of urban educational reform*. (1997). New York: Teachers College Press.

Banks, J. (1993). *An introduction to multicultural education*. Boston: Allyn and Bacon.

Barro, S., and Kolstad, A. (1987). *Who drops out of high school? Findings from high school and beyond*. Rept. CS 87-397c. Washington, DC: U.S. Department of Education, National Center for Education Statistics.

Bellah, R. N., Madsen, R., Sullivan, W. M., Swidler, A., and Tipton, S. M. (1995). *Habits of the heart*. Berkeley: University of California Press.

Berlak, H., Newmann, F. M., Adams, E., Archbald, D. A., Burgess, T., Raven, J., and Romberg, T. A. (1992). *Toward a new science of educational testing and assessment*. Albany: State University of New York Press.

Berman, P., and McLaughlin, M. (1979). *An exploratory study of school district adaptation*. Santa Monica: Rand Corporation.

Berman, P., and McLaughlin, M. (1976). Implementation of educational innovation. *Educational Forum, 40*, 344–370.

Berne, R., and Steifel, L. (1984). *The measurement of equity in school finance*. Baltimore: Johns Hopkins University Press.

Bernstein, B. (1960). Language and social class. *British Journal of Sociology, 11*, 271–276.

Bianchi, S. M. (1984). Children's progress through school: A research note. *Sociology of Education, 57*, 184–192.

Bloom, A. D. (1987). *The closing of the American mind*. New York: Simon and Schuster.

Bourdieu, P., and Passeron, J. (1990). *Reproduction in education, society, and culture*. Newbury Park, CA: Sage.

Bowles, S., and Gintis, H. (1976). *Schooling in capitalist America*. New York: Basic Books.

Bradbury, K. L., Downs, A., and Small, K. A. (1982). *Urban decline and the future of American cities.* Washington, DC: Brookings Institution.

Brown v Board of Education of Topeka, 347 U.S. 483 (1954).

Bureau of Government Research and Department of Government Services. (1992). *1992 New Jersey legislative district data book.* New Brunswick: Rutgers University.

Cibulka, J. (1987). Theories of educational budgeting: Lessons from the management of decline. *Educational Administration Quarterly, 23*(1), 7–40.

Civil Rights Act of 1964, P.L. 88-352.

Clune, W. H. (1994). The shift from equity to adequacy in school finance. *Educational Policy, 8,* 376–395.

Cohen, D. K., and Neufeld, P. (1981). The failure of high schools and the progress of education. *Daedalus, 110,* 69–90.

Cohen, D. K., and Spillane, J. P. (1993). Policy and practice: The relations between governance and instruction. In S. H. Fuhrman (Ed.), *Designing coherent education policy,* pp. 35–95. San Franscisco: Jossey-Bass.

Cole, N. S. (1990). Conceptions of educational achievement. *Educational Researcher, 19*(3), 2–7.

Coleman, J. S. (1987). Families and schools. *Educational Researcher,16,* 32–38.

Coleman, J. S., Campbell, E., Hobson, C., McPartland, J., Mood, A., Weinfield, F., and York, R. (1966). *Equality of educational opportunity.* Washington, DC: U.S. Government Printing Office.

Coley, R. J., and Goertz, M. E. (1990). *Educational standards in the 50 states: 1990.* Princeton: Educational Testing Service, Policy Information Center.

Comer, J. P. (1996). *Rallying the whole village: The Comer process for reforming education.* New York: Teachers College Press.

Coons, J. E., Clune, W. H., and Sugerman, S. D. (1970). *Private wealth and public education.* Cambridge, MA: Harvard University Press.

Cooper, B. S., and Associates. (1994). Making money matter in education: A micro-financial model for determining school-level allocations. *Journal of Education Finance, 20,* 66–87.

Cooper, B. S., Sarrel, R., and Tetenbaum, T. (1990). *Choice, funding, and pupil achievement: How urban school finance affects students—particularly those at risk.* Paper presented at the Annual Meeting of the American Educational Research Association, Boston, MA.

Council of Chief State School Officers. (1994). *State student assessment programs database, 1993–1994.* Oak Brook, IL: North Central Regional Educational Laboratory.

Dayton, J. (1993). Correlating expenditures and educational opportunity in school finance litigation: The judicial perspective. *Journal of Education Finance, 19,* 167–182.

Deal, T. E., and Kennedy, A. (1982). *Corporate cultures: The rites and rituals of corporate life.* Reading, MA: Addison-Wesley.

Decision draws mixed reaction. (June 6, 1990). *Newark Star-Ledger,* p. 1.

Delpit, L. (1995). *Other people's children: Cultural conflict in the classroom.* New York: Free Press, 1995.

Dworkin, A. G. (1987). *Teacher burnout in the public schools.* Albany: State University of New York Press.

Education Week. (1997). *Quality counts: A report card on the condition of public education in the 50 states.* Washington, DC: Author.

Ekstrom, R. B., Goertz, M. E., Pollack, J. M., and Rock, D. A. (1987). Who drops out of high school and why? Findings from a national study. In G. Natriello (Ed.), *School dropouts: Patterns and policies*, pp. 52–69. New York: Teachers College Press.

Elementary and Secondary Education Act of 1965, P.L. 89-10.

Elmore, R. F., and Fuhrman, S. H. (1995). Opportunity-to-learn standards and the state role in education. *Teachers College Record, 96*, 432–457.

Epstein, J. (1992). *School and family partnerships*. Baltimore: Center on Families, Communities, Schools, and Children's Learning.

Ferguson, R. F. (1991). Paying for public education: New evidence on how and why money matters. *Harvard Journal of Legislation, 28*, 465–499.

Firestone, W. A. (1994). Redesigning teacher salary systems for educational reform. *American Educational Research Journal, 31*, 549–574.

Firestone, W. A. (1989). Educational policy as an ecology of games. *Educational Researcher, 18*, 18–24.

Firestone, W. A., and Corbett, H. D. (1988). Planned organizational change. In N. Boyan (Ed.), *Handbook of research on educational administration*, pp. 321–340. New York: Longman Publishing.

Firestone, W. A., Fuhrman, S. H., and Kirst, M. (1993). State educational reform since 1983: Appraisal and the future. *Educational Policy, 5*, 233–250.

Florio, J. (July 15, 1990). State to demand more from schools when it pumps in more money. *Newark Star-Ledger*, sect. 1, p. 47.

Frost, L. E. (1994). At-risk statutes: Defining deviance and suppressing difference in public schools. *Journal of Law and Education, 23*, 123–165.

Fry, P. S. (1992). *Fostering children's cognitive competence through mediated learning: Frontiers and futures*. Springfield, IL: Charles C. Thomas.

Fullan, M. (1991). *The new meaning of educational change*. New York: Teachers College Press.

Fuhrman, S. H., Clune, W. H., and Elmore, R. F. (1988). Research on education reform: Lessons on the implementation of policy. *Teachers College Record, 90*, 237–258.

Gamoran, A. (1989). Resource allocation and the effects of schooling: A sociological perspective. In D. H. Monk and J. Underwood (Eds.), *Microlevel school finance: Issues and implications for policy*, pp. 207–232. Cambridge, MA: Ballinger.

General Accounting Office. (1995a). *School facilities: America's schools not designed or equipped for 21st century*. Washington, DC: Author.

General Accounting Office. (1995b). *School facilities: Conditions of America's schools*. Washington, DC: Author.

Goertz, M. E. (1995). School finance reform in New Jersey. In C. Edlefson (Ed.), *The state of school finance policy issues*, pp. 101–106, Columbus: Ohio State University, Policy Research for Ohio-Based Education.

Goertz, M. E. (1979). *Money and education in New Jersey: How far have we come?* Princeton: Educational Testing Service.

Goertz, M. E. (1978). *Money and education in New Jersey: Where did the $400 million go?* Princeton: Educational Testing Service.

Goertz, M. E., and Hannigan, J. (1978). Delivering a "thorough and efficient" education in New Jersey. *Journal of Education Finance, 4*, 46–64.

Gordon, E. W., and Yowell, C. (1994). Cultural dissonance as a risk factor in the development of students. In R. J. Rossi (Ed.), *Schools and students at risk*, pp. 51–69. New York: Teachers College Press.

Guthrie, J. W. (1980). United States school finance policy, 1955–1980. In J. W. Guthrie (Ed.), *School finance policies and practices*, pp. 3–46. Cambridge, MA: Ballinger.

Hannaway, J. (1993). Political pressure and decentralization in institutional organizations: The case of school districts. *Sociology of Education, 66*, 147–163.

Hanushek, E. A. (1989). The impact of differential expenditures on achievement. *Educational Researcher, 18*, 45–51.

Hanushek, E. A., et al. (1994). *Making schools work: Improving performance and controlling costs.* Washington, DC: The Brookings Institution.

Harper v Hunt, Opinion of the Justices, 624 Ala. So.2d 107 (1993).

Havighurst, R. J. (1965). Who are the socially disadvantaged? *Journal of Negro Education, 40*, 210–217.

Hedges, L. V., Laine, R. D., and Greenwald, R. (1994). Does money matter? A meta-analysis of studies of the effects of differential school inputs on student outcomes. *Educational Researcher, 23*, 5–14.

Hickrod, G. A. (1991). *School finance constitutional litigation: Classification of states.* Normal, IL: Illinois State University.

Hrevnack, J. (April 21, 1991). New methods needed for cleaning up old mess of an education system. *Newark Star-Ledger,* sect. 1, p. 47.

Johnson, J. (1995). *Assignment incomplete: The unfinished business of education reform.* New York: Public Agenda.

Kirst, M. W. (1977). What happens at the local level after school finance reform? *Policy Analysis, 3*, 301–324.

Kliebard, H. M. (1992). *Forging the American curriculum.* New York: Routledge.

Koffler, S. L. (1987). Assessing the impact of a state's decision to move from minimum competency testing toward higher level testing for graduation. *Educational Evaluation and Policy Analysis, 9*, 325–336.

Langer, J. A., and Allington, R. L. (1992). Curriculum research in writing and reading. In P. W. Jackson (Ed.), *Handbook of research on curriculum*, pp. 687–725. New York: Macmillan.

Lankford, H., and Wyckoff, J. (1995). Where has the money gone? An analysis of school district spending in New York. *Educational Evaluation and Policy Analysis, 17*, 195–218.

Lehne, R. (1978). *The quest for justice: The politics of school finance reform.* New York: Longman.

Levin, H. (1986). *The educational disadvantaged are still among us.* Unpublished manuscript. Stanford: Stanford University School of Education.

Levin, H. (1987). Accelerated schools for disadvantaged students. *Educational Leadership, 44*, 19–21.

Madaus, G. F. (1988). The influence of testing on the curriculum. In L. Tanner (Ed.), *Critical issues in curriculum*, pp. 83–121. Chicago: University of Chicago Press.

Massell, D., and Fuhrman, S. H. (1994). *Ten years of state education reform, 1983–1993.* New Brunswick: Consortium for Policy Research in Education.

Massell, D., Kirst, M. K., and Hoppe, M. R. (1997). *Persistence and change: School reform in nine states.* Philadelphia: Consortium for Policy Research in Education.

McAtee, S., and Thomas, Y. (1992). *Age of New Jersey public school buildings.* Trenton: Division of Finance, New Jersey State Department of Education.

McDonnell, L., and Elmore, R. (1987). Getting the job done: Alternative policy instruments. *Educational Evaluation and Policy Analysis, 9*, 133–152.

McLaughlin, M. W. (1990). The RAND change agent study revisited: Macro perspectives and micro realities. *Educational Reseacher, 19*, 11–16.

McLaughlin, M. W., Shepard, L. A., and O'Day, J. A. (1995). *Improving education through standards-based reform.* A report by the National Academy of Education Panel on Standards-Based Reform. Stanford, CA: National Academy of Education.

Minorini, P. (1994). Avoiding the limitations of the Texas and New Jersey school finance remedies with an educational adequacy theory of school reform. In S. R. Humm, B. A. Ort, M. M. Anbari, W. S. Lader, and W. S. Biel (Eds.), *Child, parent, and state: Law and policy reader,* pp. 364–373. Philadelphia: University of Pennsylvania Law Review.

Monk, D. H. (1992). Education productivity research: An update and assessment of its role in education finance reform. *Educational Evaluation and Policy Analysis, 14,* 307–331.

Montgomery, A. F., and Rossi, R. J. (1994). Becoming at risk of failure in America's schools. In R. J. Rossi (Ed.), *Schools and students at risk: Context and framework for positive change,* pp. 3–22. New York: Teachers College Press.

Montgomery, A., Rossi, R., Legters, N., McDill, E., McPartland, J., and Stringfield, S. (1993). *Educational reforms and students at risk: A review of the current state of the art.* Palo Alto: American Institutes for Research.

Morgan, M. I., Cohen, A. S., and Hershkoff, H. (1995). Establishing education program inadequacy: The Alabama example. *University of Michigan Journal of Law Reform, 28,* 559–598.

Most New Jerseyans doubt plan will aid schools or spur tax relief. (August 6, 1990). *Newark Star-Ledger,* sect 1, p. 12.

Mosteller, F. (1995). The Tennessee study of class size in early school grades. In The Center for the Future of Children (Ed.), *The future of children: Critical issues for children and youth,* pp. 113–127. Los Altos: Editor.

Moynihan, D. P. (1972). Equalizing education: In whose benefit. *The Public Interest, 29,* 71.

Mullins, D. R., and Cox, D. A. (March, 1995). Tax and expenditure limits on local governments. Washington, DC: U.S. Advisory Commission on Intergovernmental Relations. As cited in S. D. Gold, D. M. Smith, and S. B. Lawton, *Public school finance programs of the United States and Canada, 1993–1994.* Albany: American Education Finance Association and Center for the Study of the States, Nelson A. Rockefeller Institute of Government, State University of New York.

Murnane, R. J. (1995). *Staffing the nation's schools with skilled teachers.* Unpublished manuscript.

Murnane, R. J. (1991). Interpreting the evidence on ¿Does money matter?¿ *Harvard Journal on Legislation, 28,* 457–498.

Murnane, R. J., and Levy, F. (1996). *Teaching the new basic skills.* New York: Free Press.

National Center for Education Statistics. (1995). *The condition of education, 1995.* Washington, DC: U.S. Government Printing Office.

National Center for Education Statistics. (1994a). *The condition of education, 1994.* Washington, DC: U.S. Government Printing Office.

National Center for Education Statistics (1994b). *Digest of education statistics.* Washington, DC: U.S. Goverment Printing Office.

National Center for Education Statistics (1994c). *Public elementary and secondary education statistics: School year 1993–94. Early estimates.* Washington, DC: U.S. Government Printing Office.

National Commission on Excellence in Education. (1983). *A nation at risk: The imperative for educational reform.* Washington, DC: U.S. Government Printing Office.

National Council of Teachers of Mathematics. (1989). *Curriculum and evaluation standards for school mathematics.* Reston, VA: Author.

National Education Goals Panel. (1994). *The national education goals report: Building a nation of learners, 1994.* Washington, DC: Author.

Natriello, G., McDill, E. L., and Pallas, A. M. (1990). *Schooling disadvantaged children: Racing against catastrophe.* New York: Teachers College Press.

New Jersey Assembly Republican News (December 12, 1996), p.1.

New Jersey Office of Legislative Services. (July 2, 1996). *Local leeway amount subject to voter approval under governor's comprehensive plan.* Trenton: Author.

New Jersey Register. (October 5, 1992). *Thorough and efficient system of free public schools.* Subchapter 6: Programs and services for pupils at risk. 24 N.J.R. 3494.

New Jersey State Department of Education. (1994). *October 1993 grade 11 high school proficiency test (HSPTII) summary.* Trenton: Author.

New Jersey State Department of Education. (1990). *External review team report for [SN2].* Trenton: Author.

Oakes, J. (1995). Two cities' tracking and within-school segregation. *Teachers College Record, 96,* 681–690.

Odden, A. R. (1990). Class size and student achievement: Research-based policy alternatives. *Educational Evaluation and Policy Analysis, 12,* 213–228.

Odden, A. R., and Augenblick, J. (1981). *School finance reform in the states: 1981.* Report No. F81-8. Denver: Education Finance Center, Education Commission of the States.

Odden, A. R., and Dougherty, V. (1982). *State programs of school improvement: A 50-state survey.* Denver: Education Commission of the States.

Odden, A. R., and Picus, L. O. (1992). *School finance: A policy perspective.* New York: McGraw-Hill.

Odden, A. R., Monk, D., Nakib, Y., and Picus, L. O. (1995). The story of the education dollar: No academy awards and no fiscal smoking guns. *Phi Delta Kappan, 77,* 161–168.

Orfield, G. (1994a) Asking the right question. *Educational Policy, 8,* 404–413.

Orfield, G. (1994b). The Growth of segregation in American schools: Changing patterns of segregation and poverty since 1968. *Equity and Excellence in Education, 27,* 5–8.

Passow, A. H. (1984). How state education reform can improve secondary schools. Berkeley: PACE (Policy Analysis for California Education).

Passow, A. H. (1970). Deprivation and disadvantage: Nature and manifestations. In A. H. Passow (Ed.), *Deprivation and disadvantage: Nature and manifestations* (International Studies in Education, 21), pp. 15–51. Hamburg: Unesco Institute of Education.

Passow, A. H., and Elliott, D. L. (1967). The disadvantaged in depressed areas. In P. A. Witty (Ed.), *The educationally retarded and disadvantaged. The sixty-sixth yearbook of the National Society for the Study of Education, Part I,* pp. 20–39. Chicago: University of Chicago Press.

Patton, M. Q. (1990). *Qualitative evaluation and research methods,* 2d ed. Newbury Park, CA: Sage.

Peshkin, A. (1984). The imperfect union: School consolidation and community conflict. *American Journal of Education, 92*(2), 235–237.

Peterson, P. E., Rabe, B. G., and Wong, K. K. (1988). The evolution of a new corporate federalism. In N. Boyan (Ed.), *Handbook of research on educational administration,* pp. 467–486. New York: Longman.

Picus, L. O. (1994). The local impact of school finance reform in four Texas school districs. *Educational Evaluation and Policy Analysis, 16,* 391–404.

Porter, A. (1993). *Opportunity to learn.* Brief No. 7. Madison, WI: Center on Organization and Restructuring of Schools.

Public School Education Act of 1975, P.L., ch. 212.

Quality Education Act of 1990, N.J.S.A., 18a:7D1-37.

Raimondo, H. J. (1994). *How much for administration? Expenditure priorities across New Jersey school districts, FY90–91.* New Brunswick: Rutgers University, Eagleton Institute of Politics.

Ravitch, D., and Finn, C. E., Jr. (1987). *What do our 17-year-olds know?* New York: Harper.

Riley, R. (1995). The improving America's schools act and elementary and secondary education reform. *Journal of Law and Education, 24,* 513–566.

Robinson v Cahill, 62 N.J. 473 (1973). (*Robinson I*)

Robinson v Cahill, 69 N.J. 449 (1976). (*Robinson V*)

Romberg, T. A. (1992) Problematic features of the school mathematics curriculum. In P. W. Jackson (Rd.) *Handbook of research on curriculum,* pp. 749–788. New York: Macmillan.

Rose v Council for Better Education, 79-0 Ky. S.W.2d 186 (1989).

Sacks, D. (July 11, 1990). It will murder the middle class. *New York Times,* p. A14.

Salganik, L., and Celebuski, C. (1987). *Educational attainment study: Preliminary tables.* Washington, DC: Pelavin Associates.

San Antonio Independent School District v Rodriquez, 411 U.S. 1 (1973).

School debate pits city against suburbs. (December 7, 1990). *The Philadephia Inquirer,* p. B1.

Slavin, R. E. (1991). Synthesis of research on cooperative learning. *Educational Leadership, 48,* 71–82.

Slavin, R. E. (1990). General education under the regular education initiative: How must it be? *Remedial and Special Education, 11,* 40–50.

Slavin, R. E., and Braddock, J. E., III. (1993). Ability grouping: On the wrong track. *College Board Review,168,* 11–17.

Smith, M. S., Fuhrman, S. H., and O'Day, J. (1994). National curriculum standards: Are they desirable and feasible? In R. F. Elmore and S. H. Fuhrman (Eds.), *The governance of curriculum,* pp. 12–29. Arlington: Association for Supervision and Curriculum Development.

Smith, M. S., and O'Day, J. (1991). Systemic school reform. In S. H. Fuhrman and B. Malen (Eds.), *The politics of curriculum and testing,* pp. 233–267. New York: Falmer.

Tax hikes sink Florio's rating. (July 15, 1990). *Newark-Star Ledger,* sect. 1, p.1.

Tyack, D. (1974). *The one best system.* Cambridge, MA: Harvard University Press.

Underwood, J. K. (1994). School finance litigation: Legal theories, judicial activitism, and social neglect. *Journal of Education Finance, 20,* 142–162.

Verstegan, D. A. (1994). The new wave of school finance litigation. *Phi Delta Kappan, 76,* 243–250.

Viewpoint: Flawed school aid? (November 11, 1990). *Newark Star-Ledger,* sect 3, p. 2.

Wiggins, G. (1993). *Assessing student performance: Exploring the purpose and limits of testing.* San Francisco: Jossey-Bass.

Wilson, W. J. (1987). *The truly disadvantaged: The inner city, the underclass, and public policy.* Chicago: University of Chicago Press.

Wise, A. E. (1968). *Rich schools, poor schools: A promise of equal educational opportunity.* Chicago: University of Chicago Press.

Witte, J. F., and Walsh, D. J. (1990). A systematic test of the effective schools model. *Educational Evaluation and Policy Analysis, 12,* 188–212.

Wong, K. K. (1994). Governance structure, resource allocation, and equity policy. In L. Darling-Hammond (Ed.), *Review of research in education, 20,* pp. 257–290. Washington, DC: American Educational Research Association.

INDEX

ABOUT THE AUTHORS

William A. Firestone is Director of the Center for Educational Policy Analysis in New Jersey and professor of educational policy at the Graduate School of Education at Rutgers University. He was previously Director of Applied Research at Research for Better Schools in Philadelphia. He is interested in how a variety of policies affect the work of teachers. His current research activities include studies of the impact of testing on instruction. In 1974 Dr. Firestone received his Ph.D. in education and sociology from the University of Chicago.

Margaret E. Goertz is a professor in the Graduate School of Education at the University of Pennsylvania and a co-director of the Consortium for Policy Research in Education. Previously, she was Executive Director of the Education Policy Research Division of Educational Testing Service. Dr. Goertz also served as president of the American Education Finance Association. Her research focuses on issues of education finance, state education reform policies, and state and federal programs for special needs students. Her current research activities include studies of standards-based reform in education and the allocation of school-level resources. Professor Goertz received a Ph.D. in social science from the Maxwell School of Syracuse University in 1971.

Gary Natriello is Professor of Sociology and Education in the Department of Human Development at Teachers College, Columbia University. A former editor of the Section on Teaching, Learning, and Human Development of the *American Educational Research Journal*, Dr. Natriello is currently serving as the editor of the *Teachers College Record* and of the Sociology of Education Book Series at Teachers College Press. His research interests include the social organization of schools, particularly the impact of evaluation processes on teachers and students, and the educational experiences of disadvantaged youth. He is currently studying the social organization of preschool classrooms. Professor Natriello received a Ph.D. in sociology of education from Stanford University in 1979.